Shirose

Our very best wishes
for you in the future.
Good Luck!

You'll be missed

Chelsea & B.J. Windrum

By the Editors of
Favorite Recipes™ and Irena Chalmers

AWARD WINNING RECIPES

Cooking Contest Winners
From Across America

PUBLICATIONS
INTERNATIONAL, LTD.

Louis Weber, C.E.O.
Publications International, Ltd.
7373 North Cicero Avenue
Lincolnwood, Illinois 60646

Photography: Vuksanovich, Chicago, IL

Manufactured in U. S. A.

h g f e d c b a

ISBN: 0-88176-802-2

Library of Congress Catalog Card Number: 89-63614

Pictured on the front cover *(clockwise from top left)*: Chocolate Praline Layer Cake
(page 190), Rotini Salad *(page 44)* and Ginger Spicy Chicken *(page 48)*.

Pictured on the back cover *(clockwise from top left)*: Raisin-Spice Cookies *(page 154)*,
Never-Fail Fudge *(page 170)*, Peanut Blossoms *(page 158)* and Chocolate Chip & Mint
Meringue Cookies *(page 164)*.

Microwave Cooking Directions: Microwave ovens vary in wattage and power
output. Cooking times given with the microwave directions in this book may need to
be adjusted.

Contents

A WORD FROM IRENA CHALMERS

I have learned that the most popular things to collect are stamps, coins, teddy bears, dolls—and recipes. Every day millions of readers cut recipes from newspapers and magazines. These snippets are "filed" in a kitchen drawer along with all those odds and ends that are far too precious to throw away.

The editors of Favorite Recipes™ and I thought it would be far easier to find the best tried-and-true recipes if they were bound into a book—a collection of award winning recipes from cooking contests across America. We mailed hundreds of letters to chambers of commerce, state fairs, newspaper editors and food companies. Our efforts brought in Santa Claus-sized sacks of mail.

Next came the task of sorting through the mountain of recipes. For although they were all prize winners, such oddities as prune and marshmallow quiche and sharkfin cheesecake needed to be weeded out. Only the best of the best got past our collective critical eye. Our goal was to assemble a classic cookbook that included everything from appetizers to desserts. These recipes run the gamut from healthy to self-indulgent, from easy to challenging. We are confident that there is something here to please a variety of palates and lifestyles.

The contest and the champion cook's name have been included with each recipe whenever they were available. Since much of this book's charm lies in it being the work of dedicated home cooks, not professional recipe writers, we have edited the recipes just enough to make sure they are clear and accurate. I then added margin notes to entertain and inform you about such things as the background of the contests, unusual ingredients and cooking techniques. And beautiful photography adds tangible color and brings these winning recipes to life.

There are few things that give us greater pleasure in life than gathering around the table, talking, laughing and sharing food that has been prepared with loving hands. Here are recipes for many such happy times.

APPETIZERS

JUMBO SHELLS SEAFOOD FANCIES

♦ Second place winner in the Appetizing Appetizers Pasta Contest, sponsored by the North Dakota Wheat Commission and North Dakota Mill, Bismarck, North Dakota

Serves 8 to 12

> 1 (16-ounce) package uncooked jumbo-sized pasta shells
> 1 (7$^{1}/_{2}$-ounce) can crabmeat, drained, flaked and cartilage removed
> 1 (2$^{1}/_{2}$-ounce) can tiny shrimp, drained
> 1 cup (4 ounces) shredded Swiss cheese
> $^{1}/_{2}$ cup salad dressing or mayonnaise
> 2 tablespoons thinly sliced celery
> 1 tablespoon finely chopped onion
> 1 tablespoon finely chopped pimiento
> Celery leaves, for garnish

Add the shells gradually to 6 quarts of boiling salted water and cook until tender, yet firm. Drain; rinse with cold water, then drain again. Set aside, upside down, to cool. Combine the crabmeat, shrimp, cheese, dressing, celery, onion and pimiento in a small bowl. If the mixture seems too dry, add more salad dressing. Spoon the mixture into the cooled shells; cover and refrigerate until chilled. Serve the shells garnished with celery leaves.

Edith Lehr
Wishek, North Dakota

SPANAKOPITA TRIANGLES

Filo dough is of Middle Eastern origin and used to make such classic Greek dishes as spanakopita and baklava. Made of flour and water, it is essentially the same as strudel dough. Long ago it was believed that a bride-to-be was not fit for marriage until she was able to roll filo dough so thinly that her chosen groom would be able, without difficulty, to read the newspaper through it.

♦ Prize-winning recipe at the March of Dimes Gourmet Gala in Wilmington, Delaware

Makes 5 dozen appetizers

1/4 cup olive oil
1/2 cup very finely chopped onion
2 large eggs
3/4 pound feta cheese, drained and crumbled
1/2 cup very finely chopped parsley
1 teaspoon dill weed *or* 2 tablespoons chopped fresh dill
3 (10-ounce) packages frozen chopped spinach, thawed and squeezed dry
Freshly grated nutmeg to taste
Salt and freshly ground pepper to taste
1 (1-pound) package filo dough, room temperature
1 pound butter, melted

Preheat the oven to 375°F. Heat the oil in a small skillet. Add the onion and cook until translucent and golden. Beat the eggs in a large bowl with an electric mixer until they are light and lemon colored. Stir in the cooked onion, feta, parsley, dill and spinach. Season with nutmeg, salt and pepper.

Remove the filo from the package; unroll and place on a large sheet of waxed paper. Fold the filo crosswise into thirds. Use a scissors to cut along the folds into thirds. Cover with another sheet of waxed paper and a damp cloth. (Caution: Filo dries out fast if not covered.) Lay one strip of filo at a time on a flat surface and brush immediately with melted butter. Fold the strip in half lengthwise. Brush with butter again. Place a rounded teaspoonful of spinach filling on one end of the strip; fold over one corner to make a triangle. Continue folding end to end, as you would fold a flag, keeping the edges straight. Brush the top with butter. Repeat the process until all the filling is used up. Place the triangles in a single layer, seam side down, on an ungreased jelly-roll pan. Bake for about 20 minutes or until the triangles are lightly browned. Serve warm.

Jack B. Kelly and Tim Wilson

CHEESE BREAD ▶

♦ Runner-up in the Appetizers category in the Employee Cooking Contest, sponsored by Land O'Lakes, Inc.

Makes 12 to 15 slices

> 1 long loaf unsliced Vienna, French or Italian bread
> 6 ounces Land O'Lakes® Natural Cheddar Cheese
> 6 ounces Land O'Lakes® Natural Swiss Cheese
> 3/4 cup (1 1/2 sticks) Land O'Lakes® Sweet Cream Butter
> 1 tablespoon poppy seeds
> 1 tablespoon dry mustard
> 2 tablespoons chopped green onions
> 1 tablespoon lemon juice

Preheat the oven to 350°F. Make diagonal cuts in the top of the loaf, about 3 inches long, 1 1/2 inches deep and 1 1/2 inches apart. Slice the cheeses into 2 × 1/2 × 1/2-inch strips. Insert 1 strip of each cheese into each slice made in the bread. Wrap the loaf in aluminum foil, leaving the top exposed.

Melt the butter over low heat in a 1-quart saucepan. Stir in the poppy seeds, mustard, green onions and lemon juice. Drizzle the mixture over the bread. Bake for about 35 minutes or until the cheese melts. Slice the bread and serve warm.

Karilyn Schrankler
Arden Hills, Minnesota

To check if an egg has been hard-cooked, spin it like a top. If it spins on its end, it is cooked; if it turns on its side, it is raw.

SPRING SANDWICHES FOR MARY

♦ Prize-winning recipe at the March of Dimes Gourmet Gala in Lexington, Kentucky

Makes 24 appetizers

> 1/2 loaf day-old white bread, unsliced
> 10 anchovy fillets, rinsed and finely chopped
> 2 tablespoons Dijon-style mustard
> 4 hard-cooked eggs, finely chopped
> 1/4 cup finely chopped fresh dill *or* 1/4 cup combined finely chopped dill, parsley and chives
> 1/8 teaspoon freshly ground black pepper
> 2 tablespoons butter
> 2 tablespoons vegetable oil

(continued)

Trim the crusts from the bread; cut into twelve ⅛-inch-thick slices. Mash the chopped anchovies, mustard, eggs, herbs and pepper in a small bowl. (The mixture should be quite smooth.) Spread egg mixture thickly on 6 of the bread slices. Top each slice with another slice of bread and lightly press them together.

Melt the butter and oil in a large skillet over medium heat. When the foam subsides, add the sandwiches, 2 or 3 at a time. Fry for 2 to 3 minutes on each side or until crisp and golden brown. Drain on paper towels. Cut into quarters and serve hot.

H. Foster Pettit

MUSHROOMS STUFFED WITH CRABMEAT

♦ Fifth place winner at the Mushroom Cook-Off, sponsored by the Pennsylvania Fresh Mushroom Program, Kennett Square, Pennsylvania

Makes 8 appetizer or 4 first-course servings

  16 large mushroom caps
  ⅓ cup (⅔ stick) butter, melted
1½ cups flaked crabmeat
  2 eggs, lightly beaten
  ½ cup finely chopped green onions
  ½ cup soft bread crumbs, divided
  3 tablespoons mayonnaise
  2 teaspoons fresh lemon juice
  2 tablespoons butter, chilled

Preheat the oven to 375°F. Grease a large baking dish. Dip the mushroom caps into the melted butter, then place them, rounded side down, in the prepared dish. Combine the crabmeat, eggs, green onions, ¼ cup of the bread crumbs, the mayonnaise and lemon juice in a medium-sized bowl and blend thoroughly. Fill the mushroom caps with this mixture. Sprinkle with the remaining ¼ cup bread crumbs and dot with the chilled butter. Bake for 15 minutes or until the crumbs on top are golden brown. Serve hot.

Audrey Snyder
Hatfield, Pennsylvania

MICROWAVED MEXICAN FRITTATA

♦ Third place winner in the Kansas Egg Recipe Contest, sponsored by the Kansas Poultry Association, the Kansas State Board of Agriculture and the American Egg Board

Makes 10 appetizer or 5 main-course servings

2 tablespoons butter or margarine
3 green onions, sliced
1 (12-ounce) can Mexican-style corn, drained
1 (4-ounce) can chopped green chilies, drained
¼ teaspoon chili powder
¼ teaspoon salt
⅛ teaspoon ground cumin
  Ground red pepper
¼ cup all-purpose flour
5 eggs
½ cup sour cream
1 cup (4 ounces) shredded Cheddar cheese
1 cup (4 ounces) shredded Monterey Jack cheese
⅓ cup salsa
  Tortilla chips (optional)
  Ripe olives (optional)

MICROWAVE COOKING DIRECTIONS:
Put the butter in a 10-inch microwavable quiche or pie dish and microwave on High (100% power) for 30 seconds. Add the green onions, corn, chilies, chili powder, salt, cumin and pepper; mix well. Microwave on High for 3 minutes or until the green onions are tender, stirring after 1½ minutes. Stir in the flour and mix until smooth.

Using a wire whisk, beat the eggs and the sour cream in a medium-sized bowl until thoroughly blended, then stir into the corn mixture. Add the cheeses and mix well. Microwave on Medium (50% power) for 20 minutes or until the egg mixture is almost set but still moist in the center, rotating the dish a quarter turn every 5 minutes. Let stand on the counter for 10 minutes. Cut into wedges to serve, spooning a little salsa over each serving. Tastes great served with tortilla chips and ripe olives.

Janice Blansit
Kansas City, Kansas

Canned Chilies

Canned chilies should be rinsed in cold water before using. Much of the "fire" is in the seeds and canning liquid. The canners who pack chilies rate their hotness on a scale of 1 to 200—with 1 being the mildest. A jalapeño chili, hot enough to burn your mouth, bring tears to your eyes and make your hair curl, rates 15 on this scale! Taste canned chilies very warily if you are a novice.

FRESH TOMATO PASTA ANDREW

♦ First place winner in the California Fresh Market Tomato Advisory Board Contest, Los Angeles, California

Serves 4 as a first course

> 1 pound fresh tomatoes, cut into wedges
> 1 cup packed fresh basil leaves
> 2 cloves garlic, chopped
> 2 tablespoons olive oil
> 8 ounces Camenzola cheese *or* 6 ounces ripe Brie plus
>   2 ounces Stilton cheese, each cut into small pieces
>   Salt and white pepper to taste
> 4 ounces uncooked angel hair pasta, vermicelli or
>   other thin pasta
>   Freshly grated Parmesan cheese

Place the tomato wedges, basil, garlic and oil in a food processor or blender; pulse on and off until the ingredients are roughly chopped, but not pureed. Combine the tomato mixture and Camenzola cheese in a large bowl and season with salt and pepper. Cook the pasta in rapidly boiling salted water until tender, yet firm; drain. Add the hot pasta to the tomato sauce and toss until the cheese melts. Serve topped with Parmesan cheese.

Dahlia Haas
Los Angeles, California

PEAMOLE

♦ Prize winner at the Great Harvest Split Pea & Lentil Cook-Off, Moscow, Idaho

Makes 2¹/₄ cups

> 2 cups water
> 1 cup green split peas
> 1 teaspoon salt, divided
> ¹/₂ cup sour cream
> ¹/₃ cup wine vinegar
> 1 tablespoon lemon juice
> 1 tablespoon dehydrated onion *or* 2 tablespoons very
>   finely chopped fresh onion
> ¹/₂ teaspoon garlic powder
>   Few dashes of Tabasco pepper sauce

Combine the water, split peas and ½ teaspoon of the salt in a medium-sized saucepan. Bring to a boil; cover, reduce the heat and simmer for 1 hour. Remove from the heat and allow to cool to room temperature. Puree the peas in a blender or food processor until smooth. Add the sour cream, vinegar, lemon juice, onion, garlic powder, the remaining ½ teaspoon salt and the pepper sauce to the cooled puree; blend well. Cover; refrigerate until thoroughly chilled. Serve as a dip with tortilla chips or as a substitute for guacamole with other dishes.

Note: The peamole stores well, covered, in the refrigerator; it does not darken like guacamole.

Zoe Eckblad
Moscow, Idaho

THATCHED ROOF APPETIZER

♦ Second prize winner in "The Secret's in the Soup" Recipe Contest, sponsored by Thomas J. Lipton, Inc.

Makes about 1 quart

  1 pound ground beef
  1 (10-ounce) can tomatoes with green chilies, undrained
 ½ cup water
  1 envelope Lipton® Onion Recipe Soup Mix
 ¼ teaspoon pepper
    Dash of hot pepper sauce
  1 (16-ounce) can refried beans
 1½ cups (6 ounces) shredded Monterey Jack or mozzarella cheese
 ¼ cup sliced pimiento-stuffed green olives
    Corn tortilla or nacho chips, for serving

Brown the ground beef in a large skillet; drain off the excess fat and discard it. Stir in the undrained tomatoes, water, soup mix, pepper and hot pepper sauce. Bring to a boil, then reduce the heat and simmer, uncovered, stirring occasionally for 20 minutes or until the sauce is thickened. Stir in the beans and heat through. Turn the mixture into a 1½-quart casserole or serving bowl and top with the cheese and olives. Serve warm with corn tortilla chips.

Karen Hill Murphy
Houston, Texas

Refried beans are served at almost every meal in Mexico. However, they are only fried once. The "re-" prefix is simply an imperfect translation, implying that the beans should be thoroughly fried after the preliminary cooking.

Clarifying Butter

Clarified butter is what remains after removing protein and other substances from butter. It is simple to make and has the advantage of cooking at high temperatures without burning. Melt the butter over low heat. Skim off the white foam that forms on top, then strain the clear, golden clarified butter through cheesecloth into a container. Discard the milky residue at the bottom of the pan. You can make a large quantity of clarified butter at a time. It will keep, covered, in the refrigerator for up to 2 months.

SCAMPI ALLA "FIREMAN CHEF" ▶

♦ Finalist in the Gilroy Garlic Festival Recipe Contest, Gilroy, California. Courtesy of the Gilroy Garlic Festival Association's *Garlic Lover's Cookbook.*

Makes 8 appetizer servings

> 16 large prawns (about 1¹/₂ pounds), peeled and deveined
> ¹/₃ cup clarified butter
> 4 tablespoons very finely chopped garlic
> 6 green onions, thinly sliced
> ¹/₄ cup dry white wine
> Juice of 1 lemon (about 2 tablespoons)
> 8 large sprigs fresh parsley, very finely chopped
> Salt and freshly ground pepper to taste
> Lemon slices and parsley sprigs, for garnish

Rinse the prawns and set aside. Heat the clarified butter in a large skillet over medium heat. Cook the garlic for 1 to 2 minutes or until softened, being careful not to let it brown. Add the prawns, green onions, wine and lemon juice and cook until the prawns turn pink and firm, 1 to 2 minutes on each side. Be careful not to overcook. At the last minute, add the chopped parsley and season with salt and pepper. Serve the scampi on individual shell-shaped or small gratin dishes, garnished with a slice or two of lemon and a fresh parsley sprig.

Jim Neil
Gilroy, California

FALL HARVEST POPCORN

♦ First place winner in the Appetizers category in the annual recipe contest sponsored by the *Reflector-Chronicle*, Abilene, Kansas

Makes 2¹/₂ quarts

> 2 quarts freshly popped popcorn, unsalted
> 2 (1³/₄-ounce) cans shoestring potatoes (3 cups)
> 1 cup salted mixed nuts
> 4 tablespoons (¹/₂ stick) butter or margarine, melted
> 1 teaspoon dill weed
> 1 teaspoon Worcestershire sauce
> ¹/₂ teaspoon lemon-pepper seasoning
> ¹/₄ teaspoon garlic powder
> ¹/₄ teaspoon onion powder

(continued)

Preheat the oven to 325°F. Combine the popcorn, shoestring potatoes and nuts in a large roasting pan. Set aside. Combine the butter, dill, Worcestershire sauce, lemon-pepper seasoning, garlic powder and onion powder in a small bowl; pour over the popcorn mixture, stirring until evenly coated. Bake for 8 to 10 minutes, stirring once. Cool completely; store in airtight containers.

Peggy Meuli
Hope, Kansas

The average American does not eat even one whole artichoke a year. Seven-eighths of one is what it works out to be. Those we do eat are all grown in and around Castroville, California. There is even a big, barnlike place in Castroville built to resemble a giant artichoke where they serve artichokes prepared a hundred different ways.

ARTICHOKE CRAB PUFFS

♦ Prize winner at the Castroville Artichoke Festival Recipe Contest, Castroville, California

Makes 4 dozen appetizers

> 2 dozen baby artichokes
> Lemon juice
> 8 tablespoons (1 stick) butter, divided
> 1 small shallot, very finely chopped
> 1 clove garlic, very finely chopped
> 1 cup milk
> 1 teaspoon dried tarragon
> 1 cup all-purpose flour
> 2 tablespoons Dijon-style mustard
> 1/4 teaspoon ground white pepper
> Dash of ground red pepper
> 4 eggs
> 1 cup (4 ounces) shredded Swiss cheese, divided
> 1/2 pound crabmeat, picked over to remove traces of shell and chopped

Trim the artichokes by cutting the bottoms flat and pulling off outer leaves until the leaves are yellow with pale green tips. Snip off the green tips. Put the artichokes in a large bowl of water; add lemon juice to prevent darkening.

Bring water to a boil in a large pot; add the artichokes. Cook, uncovered, for 15 minutes. Remove the artichokes and drain upside down on paper towels. Meanwhile, melt 1 tablespoon of the butter in a large saucepan; add the shallot and cook until translucent. Add the garlic and cook another minute. Add the remaining 7 tablespoons butter, the milk and tarragon; bring to a boil. Remove from the heat; add the flour all at once. Cook and stir over medium-low heat for about 2 minutes or until the mixture leaves the sides of the pan and forms a ball. Remove from the heat and stir in the mustard, and white and red peppers. Beat in the eggs, one at a time, until each egg is incorporated and the mixture is smooth. (This can be done in a food processor.) Fold in 3/4 cup of the cheese and the crabmeat.

Preheat the oven to 375°F. Grease a baking sheet. Halve the artichokes lengthwise; remove and discard the fuzzy choke. Using a spoon or a pastry tube, stuff the artichoke halves generously with the crab mixture. Arrange on the prepared sheet and sprinkle with the remaining 1/4 cup cheese. Bake for about 30 minutes or until golden brown. Remove from the oven; puncture each puff with a knife or skewer to release the steam. Serve warm.

Hy Tran
Palo Alto, California

SALSA FOR SIX

♦ Prize winner at the Mayor's Great American Chile Championship Cook-Off, Santa Fe Convention & Visitors Bureau, Santa Fe, New Mexico

Serves 6

    2 (17-ounce) cans crushed tomatoes
  2/3 cup water
  1/4 cup chopped jalapeño peppers*
    1 green onion, finely chopped (including 2 inches of
        green stem)
    1 tablespoon finely chopped yellow onion
    2 teaspoons dried cilantro
    2 teaspoons crushed red chile pepper
1 1/2 teaspoons salt
    1 teaspoon garlic powder
  1/2 teaspoon dried basil
  1/2 teaspoon black pepper
  1/4 teaspoon ground cumin

Combine the ingredients and blend thoroughly. Let stand for several hours at room temperature and refrigerate before serving.

Wear rubber gloves when working with hot peppers and wash your hands in warm soapy water. Avoid touching your face or eyes.

Don Stroud
Chef, Little Chief Grill
Santa Fe, New Mexico

There is no one definition of salsa, for it can be so hot that it will sear the roof of your mouth or so mild that you can use it as a dipping sauce. Its ingredients vary depending on the region in which it is made and on the use for which it is intended. It does, however, always contain tomatoes and chilies in some form or another.

SOUTHWEST APPETIZER CHEESECAKE

♦ Winner in the Philly "Hall of Fame" Recipe Contest, sponsored by Philadelphia Brand® Cream Cheese

Makes 10 to 12 appetizer servings

- ²/₃ cup finely crushed tortilla chips
- 2 tablespoons margarine, melted
- 1 cup cottage cheese
- 3 (8-ounce) packages cream cheese, softened
- 4 eggs
- 10 ounces shredded sharp natural Cheddar cheese
- 1 (4-ounce) can chopped green chilies, drained
- 1 (8-ounce) container sour cream
- 1 (8-ounce) container jalapeño-Cheddar gourmet dip
- 1 cup chopped tomatoes
- ¹/₂ cup chopped green onions
- ¹/₄ cup pitted ripe olive slices

Preheat the oven to 325°F. Combine the tortilla chips and margarine and press the mixture onto the bottom of a 9-inch springform pan. Bake for 15 minutes. Meanwhile, place the cottage cheese in a blender or food processor. Cover and process on high speed until smooth. In the large bowl of an electric mixer, combine the cottage cheese and cream cheese, mixing at medium speed until well blended. Add the eggs, one at a time, mixing well after each addition. Blend in the Cheddar cheese and chilies. Pour the mixture over the baked crust. Return the pan to the oven and bake for 1 hour.

Combine the sour cream and dip; mix thoroughly. Spread the mixture over the hot cheesecake; return to the oven and continue baking for 10 minutes. Remove from the oven and let cool slightly. Loosen the cake from the rim of the pan; cool completely before removing the rim. Refrigerate the cheesecake until ready to serve. Top with the tomatoes, green onions and olives before serving.

Debbie Vanni
Libertyville, Illinois

ineapples need 18 months from the moment they are planted until the first harvest is ready. The second harvest from the same plant will ripen in another 12 months. This constitutes the total life cycle of a pineapple plant. At maturity, it is replaced with another.

PINEAPPLE SWEET-SOUR SPARERIBS

♦ First prize winner in the Appetizer category in "Generations of Good Cooking," an employee contest sponsored by Dole Packaged Foods Company

Makes 16 appetizer servings

    1 (8-ounce) can Dole® Pineapple Chunks in Syrup
    3 to 4 pounds lean spareribs, cut into 2-inch pieces
    4 tablespoons soy sauce, divided
    3 tablespoons cornstarch
      Vegetable oil
    2 cloves garlic, pressed
    1 (2-inch) piece fresh ginger, peeled and grated
    1 cup cider vinegar
    3/4 cup packed brown sugar
    1/3 cup water
    1 teaspoon salt

Drain the pineapple, reserving the syrup. Rub the ribs with 2 tablespoons of the soy sauce and the cornstarch. Pour just enough oil into a large skillet to cover the bottom; heat over medium heat. Add the ribs and brown thoroughly on all sides. Combine the reserved syrup, the remaining 2 tablespoons soy sauce, the garlic, ginger, vinegar, brown sugar, water and salt in a large saucepan. Cut the ribs into 2-rib pieces; add to the saucepan and bring to a boil. Reduce the heat; cover and simmer for 1 hour, stirring occasionally. Spoon off any excess oil. Stir in the pineapple; heat just through and serve.

Esther L. Chee
Honolulu, Hawaii

SOUPS & SALADS

Soups

The list of famous
German sausages is long
and mouth-watering:
frankfurters, bratwurst,
liverwurst, knockwurst
and weisswurst are just
a few. All are made
with different
combinations of
ingredients, including
beef, veal, pork and
seasonings. Always be
sure to pierce the skin
with the point of a
paring knife before
cooking, or the sausage
will burst through the
skin.

OLD-FASHIONED GERMAN SAUSAGE & LENTIL SOUP

♦ Prize winner at the Great Harvest Split Pea & Lentil Cook-Off, Moscow, Idaho

Makes about 8 servings

2 cups uncooked lentils
2 quarts chicken broth or water
1 pound German sausage* or ham hock, cut crosswise
    into slices
1 medium-size onion, finely chopped
3 carrots, sliced
2 ribs celery, sliced
2 (14½-ounce) cans stewed tomatoes
2 small potatoes, peeled and diced
1 bay leaf
1½ teaspoons salt
½ teaspoon dried thyme
    Pinch of dried rosemary
    Freshly ground pepper to taste
1 tablespoon vinegar
    Grated Parmesan cheese (optional)

Rinse and drain the lentils. Bring the chicken broth to a boil in a large saucepan over high heat. Add the lentils and sausage. Reduce the heat; cover and simmer for 1

(continued)

If you like, you can cook the sausage first to remove some of the fat.

hour. Add the onion, carrots, celery, tomatoes, potatoes, bay leaf, salt, thyme and rosemary; simmer for 1 hour or until the vegetables are tender. (If the soup becomes too thick, add more broth or water.) Season with pepper and stir in the vinegar. Remove and discard the bay leaf. Sprinkle each serving with Parmesan cheese.

Angie Flynn
Pullman, Washington

Freezing Soups

1. Before freezing, refrigerate the soup until the fat rises to the surface. Skim the fat and discard bones, bay leaves or any other ingredients that will not be eaten.

2. Divide the soup into portions to serve two, four or more, depending on the number of people you are most likely to be feeding at one time.

3. To save freezer space, store the soup in self-sealing plastic bags, stacking them in the freezer like pages in a book. Be sure to label each bag with its contents.

MICROWAVED GREEN ONION AND PASTA SOUP

♦ Runner-up in the Savory Soups Pasta Contest, sponsored by the North Dakota Wheat Commission and North Dakota Mill, Bismarck, North Dakota

Makes 4 to 5 servings

> 2 cups water
> 1 cup uncooked ring or shell macaroni
> 2 tablespoons butter
> 1 cup finely chopped green onions, including green tops
> 3 cups milk
> 1 tablespoon instant beef bouillon
> 1/4 teaspoon pepper
> 1/8 teaspoon ground nutmeg
> 1/2 cup chopped American cheese (about 4 to 5 slices)

MICROWAVE COOKING DIRECTIONS:
Place the water in a microwavable 1-quart bowl or measuring cup. Microwave on High (100% power) until boiling. Add the macaroni and microwave on High until boiling again. Stir once and let stand while you prepare the remaining ingredients.

Place the butter in a microwavable 4-quart bowl and microwave on High just until melted. Add the green onions and microwave on High for 3 minutes, stirring once. Slowly stir in the milk, then the bouillon, pepper, nutmeg and cheese. Microwave on High for about 5 minutes or until almost boiling. Drain the macaroni and add it to the soup. Microwave on Low (30% power) for about 3 minutes. Serve with garlic toast or crisp bread sticks.

Gloria Porter
Grandin, North Dakota

CURRIED SWEET POTATO & BRUSSELS SPROUT SOUP

♦ Winner in the Most Original Recipe category at the Brussels Sprouts Harvest Festival in Santa Cruz, California

Makes 1¹/₂ gallons

    8 tablespoons (1 stick) butter, divided
    3 cups chopped onions
    2 teaspoons grated fresh ginger
    2 teaspoons very finely chopped garlic
    1 tablespoon salt, divided
    1 tablespoon pepper, divided
    2 tablespoons curry powder
  ¹/₂ teaspoon ground cinnamon
    8 cups cubed uncooked sweet potatoes
    8 cups water
    1 bay leaf
  ¹/₂ teaspoon dried thyme
    8 cups chopped brussels sprouts (about 5 pounds)
    2 tablespoons white wine
    4 cups milk
    1 cup sour cream
    1 tablespoon tamari
    1 tablespoon lemon juice

Melt 4 tablespoons of the butter in a large pot. Add the onions, ginger, garlic, 1¹/₂ teaspoons of the salt and 1¹/₂ teaspoons of the pepper; cook over medium heat until the onions are translucent. Add the curry powder and cinnamon; cook and stir for 2 minutes. Add the sweet potatoes, water, bay leaf and thyme. Cover and cook over medium-high heat until the potatoes are soft. Remove from the heat.

In a second large pot, melt the remaining 4 tablespoons butter. Add the sprouts, wine, remaining 1¹/₂ teaspoons salt and 1¹/₂ teaspoons pepper; cook until the sprouts are tender.

Place the potato mixture into a food processor or blender. Process until smooth and add to the second pot. Process the milk, sour cream, tamari and lemon juice in the food processor or blender with a small amount of hot water; add to the pot. Cook until just heated through; do not boil.

Amy Sherman and Cindy Lepore
Seychelles Restaurant
Santa Cruz, California

For those who consider brussels sprouts an acquired taste, the Santa Cruz Brussels Sprouts Harvest Festival offers sprout tostadas, sprout pizza, sprout water taffy, tempura sprouts and chocolate-covered sprouts. And for those still not tempted, the festival has a sprout tossing contest and a "Sprout-In-One" competition for golf buffs.

Tamari is a thick, dark, pungent sauce made from soybeans. Japanese in origin, it is available at health food stores and in the imported (Oriental) section of some supermarkets.

PICANTE ONION SOUP ▸

♦ Grand Prize winner in the Pace® Picante Sauce ".Pick Up the Pace" Recipe Contest, sponsored by Pace Foods, Inc.

Makes about 5 cups

> 3 cups thinly sliced onions
> 1 clove garlic, very finely chopped
> 4 tablespoons (¹/₂ stick) butter or margarine
> 2 cups tomato juice
> 1 (10¹/₂-ounce) can condensed beef broth
> 1 soup can water
> ¹/₂ cup Pace® Picante Sauce
> 1 cup unseasoned croutons
> 1 cup (4 ounces) shredded Monterey Jack cheese

Place the onions, garlic and butter in a 3-quart saucepan. Cook over medium-low heat for about 20 minutes, stirring frequently, until the onions are tender and golden brown. Stir in the tomato juice, broth, water and picante sauce; bring to a boil. Reduce the heat and simmer, uncovered, for 20 minutes. Ladle the soup into bowls and sprinkle with the croutons and cheese. Serve with bread sticks and additional picante sauce on the side.

Joyce Lee Sproul
Pembroke Pines, Florida

Stock-Making Basics

1. Place the meat and bones in a soup pot and cover with cold water.

2. Heat the water slowly to a boil without stirring. Use a ladle to remove the scum as it collects on the surface of the water.

3. When boiling, add the vegetables and seasonings of your choice; add salt sparingly. Reduce the heat and simmer gently, partially covered, for at least 2 hours.

4. Strain the stock through dampened cheesecloth. To remove the fat from the stock, cover and refrigerate. The fat will solidify on the surface for easy removal.

BASIL VEGETABLE SOUP ▸

♦ Prize-winning recipe at the March of Dimes Gourmet Gala in New York, New York

Serves 10 to 12

> 1 (9-ounce) package frozen cut green beans, slightly thawed
> 1 (15-ounce) can cooked white beans, undrained
> 3 medium-size carrots, cut into thin rounds
> 3 medium-size zucchini, cut into rounds
> 2 quarts beef and/or chicken broth, preferably homemade
> 2 cloves garlic, very finely chopped
> Salt and pepper to taste
> 1 cup uncooked vermicelli
> ¹/₂ cup tightly packed fresh basil leaves, very finely chopped
> Grated Parmesan cheese
> Chopped parsley, for garnish

(continued)

Combine the green and white beans, carrots, zucchini, broth and garlic in a deep soup pot. Bring to a boil, then reduce the heat. Cover and simmer until the carrots are tender. Season with salt and pepper. Add the vermicelli and simmer until the pasta is tender, yet firm. (If you prefer, the pasta may be cooked separately and added to the soup.) Add the basil and continue simmering until the basil is completely tender. Taste for seasoning and serve in deep bowls. Sprinkle each serving with cheese and parsley.

Hope Lange

Cannellini beans are cultivated white beans used extensively in Italian cooking. Great Northern beans may be substituted.

BETTY JAYNE'S GARLIC SOUP

♦ Finalist in the Gilroy Garlic Festival Recipe Contest, Gilroy, California. Courtesy of the Gilroy Garlic Festival Association's *Garlic Lover's Cookbook.*

Makes 8 cups

¼ cup olive oil
30 large cloves fresh garlic, chopped
 2 (16-ounce) cans chicken broth
 2 cups water
 2 (15-ounce) cans cannellini beans, undrained
 1 teaspoon salt
 1 teaspoon black pepper
 2 bay leaves
 1 fresh jalapeño pepper, seeded and chopped*
 1 cup heavy cream
12 slices French bread
   Grated Parmesan cheese

Heat the oil in a large saucepan over medium heat. Add the garlic and cook until soft and golden. Add the chicken broth, water, beans, salt, black pepper, bay leaves and jalapeño pepper; simmer for 5 minutes. Pour the mixture into a food processor or blender and process until smooth. Return the soup to the saucepan; stir in the cream and cook until just heated through. Do not allow it to boil. Meanwhile, heat the broiler. Toast the bread lightly under the broiler. Sprinkle the toasted slices with the cheese and broil for 3 minutes or until the cheese is golden and bubbly. Serve the toast in the soup.

Wear rubber gloves when working with hot peppers and wash your hands in warm soapy water. Avoid touching your face or eyes.

Betty Jayne Jones
Longview, Washington

CHILLY CUCUMBER SOUP

♦ First prize winner in "The Secret's in the Soup" Recipe Contest, sponsored by Thomas J. Lipton, Inc.

Makes about 6 servings

   2 tablespoons butter or margarine
   2 tablespoons all-purpose flour
   4 large cucumbers, peeled, seeded and finely chopped
      (about 3¹/₂ cups)
 ¹/₄ cup finely chopped parsley
 ¹/₄ cup finely chopped celery leaves
   1 envelope Lipton® Golden Onion Recipe Soup Mix
   2 cups water
   2 cups light cream or half-and-half

Melt the butter in a large saucepan. Stir in the flour and cook over medium heat, stirring constantly, for 3 minutes. Add the cucumbers, parsley and celery leaves. Cook over low heat for 8 minutes or until the cucumbers are tender. Stir in the soup mix blended with the water. Bring to a boil, then reduce the heat, cover and simmer for 15 minutes. Remove from the heat and set aside to cool. When cooled, puree the soup mixture in a food processor or blender. Stir in the cream; cover and refrigerate. Serve the soup cold.

Joel Stephens
Nashville, Tennessee

Here is a valuable tip to keep in mind in case you should find yourself dying of thirst on a desert island: Eat a cucumber. It is 96 percent water and maintains a lower temperature than the air around it. In fact, it was to have a year-round supply of cucumbers that hothouses were first built.

SHAKER CHICKEN AND NOODLE SOUP

♦ Runner-up in the Savory Soups Pasta Contest, sponsored by the North Dakota Wheat Commission and North Dakota Mill, Bismarck, North Dakota

Makes 15 servings

  13 cups chicken broth, divided
 ¹/₄ cup dry vermouth
   4 tablespoons (¹/₂ stick) butter
   1 cup heavy cream
   1 (12-ounce) package frozen egg noodles
1¹/₂ cups water
 ³/₄ cup all-purpose flour
   2 cups diced cooked chicken
      Salt and pepper to taste
 ¹/₄ cup finely chopped parsley, for garnish   *(continued)*

Combine 1 cup of the broth, the vermouth and butter in a small saucepan. Bring to a boil and cook until the liquid has reduced to 1/4 cup and is syrupy in consistency. Stir in the cream; set aside.

Bring the remaining 12 cups broth to a boil in a large saucepan. Add the noodles and cook until they are just tender. Combine the water and flour, stirring until smooth; add to the noodle mixture. Boil for 2 minutes, stirring constantly. Stir in the reserved cream mixture and the chicken. Season with salt and pepper. Heat just to serving temperature; do not allow the soup to boil. Sprinkle with parsley and serve.

Note: This soup freezes well.

Lorraine Bourgois
Bismarck, North Dakota

A good soup pot is one that is heavy and conducts and distributes heat evenly. Copper is the ideal metal, though its cost puts it out of range for most cooks. Good alternatives are Calphalon, aluminum, or stainless steel with a copper or aluminum core.

NOODLE-BROCCOLI-CHEESE ▶ SOUP

♦ Fourth place winner in the Savory Soups Pasta Contest, sponsored by the North Dakota Wheat Commission and North Dakota Mill, Bismarck, North Dakota

Makes 8 servings

  2 tablespoons butter
 1/2 cup finely chopped onion
  1 clove garlic, finely chopped
  4 cups chicken broth
  6 ounces uncooked fine or thin noodles
  1 (16-ounce) package frozen broccoli cut spears, partially thawed
  4 cups milk
 12 ounces American and/or Cheddar cheese, shredded
    Salt and pepper to taste
    Croutons and fresh parsley sprigs (optional)

Heat the butter in a large soup pot. Add the onion and garlic and cook until soft. Add the broth and bring to a boil. Stir in the noodles and cook until almost tender. Add the broccoli and milk; heat thoroughly, but do not allow to boil. Stir in the cheese and continue heating until it melts. Season with salt and pepper. Serve the soup immediately. Garnish with croutons and parsley sprigs.

Bev Helm
Denhoff, North Dakota

*K*idney beans can be used interchangeably with pintos and are available dried and canned. They play a controversial role in the preparation of chili—some think chili should contain beans, while others insist that genuine chili should never include them.

SANTA FE TRAIL CHILE

♦ Prize winner at the Mayor's Great American Chile Championship Cook-Off, Santa Fe Convention & Visitors Bureau, Santa Fe, New Mexico

Serves 12

1/4 cup vegetable oil
1 pound pork butt, cut into cubes
1 pound beef chuck or ball tip, cut into cubes
1 pound ground pork
1 pound lean ground beef
2 medium-size yellow onions, diced
3 green bell peppers, diced
2 ribs celery, diced
1/2 pound fresh or frozen chopped green chiles
1 (12-ounce) bottle beer
2 cups cooked pinto beans
1 (16-ounce) can kidney beans, undrained
1 (8-ounce) can tomatoes, undrained, diced
1 (8-ounce) can tomato sauce
Salt to taste
1/3 cup red chile powder
3 tablespoons finely chopped fresh garlic
2 tablespoons dried oregano
1 tablespoon ground cumin

Heat the oil in a large skillet until medium-hot. Add the pork butt and beef chuck and sear over medium heat until a rich dark color. Add the ground pork and ground beef; cook until browned. Drain and discard the fat. Add the onions, bell peppers, celery and green chiles to the skillet and stir to combine; pour in the beer. Cover and simmer for 20 minutes over very low heat. Add the pinto and kidney beans, tomatoes and tomato sauce. Season with salt. Stir in the red chile powder, garlic, oregano and cumin; simmer 1 hour more, adding water if necessary to thin. Cool; cover and refrigerate overnight. (The chile tastes best the next day.)

Scott Almy
Chef, Hotel St. Francis
Santa Fe, New Mexico

BARNSTORMERS' CHILI

♦ Prize-winning recipe from the Golden Chili Pepper Awards,
sponsored by the American Spice Trade Association

Makes 8 to 10 servings

 1/3 cup instant minced onion
   2 teaspoons instant minced garlic
   6 tablespoons water
   2 tablespoons vegetable oil
   3 pounds boneless beef top round, sirloin or chuck,
      cut into 1/2-inch cubes
 3/4 cup chili powder
   1 (12-ounce) can beer
   1 (8-ounce) can tomato sauce
   2 tablespoons ground cumin
 1/2 teaspoon dried oregano, crushed
 1/2 teaspoon salt
 1/2 teaspoon ground black pepper
 1/4 teaspoon ground coriander
 1/4 teaspoon dried marjoram, crushed
 1/8 teaspoon ground cloves
 1/8 teaspoon dry mustard
 1/8 teaspoon ground red pepper
 1/2 to 1 cup beef broth
   1 tablespoon tequila

Combine the onion, garlic and water in a small bowl and
let stand for about 10 minutes to soften. Heat the oil in a
large skillet until hot. Add half of the beef; cook and stir
for about 5 minutes or until browned on all sides.
Remove the beef from the pan using a slotted spoon.
Add the remaining beef; cook and stir until browned.
Return all the beef to the pan; reduce the heat to
medium. Add the softened onion and garlic; cook and
stir for about 5 minutes or until tender. Add the chili
powder and stir to coat the meat. Stir in the beer, tomato
sauce, cumin, oregano, salt, black pepper, coriander,
marjoram, cloves, mustard and red pepper. Bring to a
boil; reduce the heat, cover and simmer until the beef is
tender. (This will take about 30 minutes for top round or
sirloin and about 1 hour for chuck.) Add enough beef
broth to thin the chili to the consistency you prefer.
Remove from the heat; stir in the tequila and serve.

Richard and Tammy Rutherford
Palmdale, California

Salads

TROPICAL CHICKEN SALAD

♦ Third prize winner in the Savory category of the International Association of Cooking Professionals Recipe Contest, sponsored by Coco Lopez® Cream of Coconut, a product of Borden, Inc.

Makes 4 servings

>   Tropical Salad Dressing (recipe follows)
> 3 cups cubed cooked chicken
> 3/4 cup coarsely chopped celery
> 3/4 cup seedless red or green grape halves
> 3/4 cup coarsely chopped macadamia nuts or toasted almonds
>   Lettuce leaves, for serving
>   Sliced strawberries, kiwifruit and avocado, for garnish
>   Toasted coconut flakes, for garnish

Prepare the Tropical Salad Dressing. Combine the chicken, celery, grapes and nuts in a large bowl; stir in 1 cup of the dressing. Cover and refrigerate to allow the flavors to blend. Mound the salad on a platter or individual plates lined with lettuce leaves. Garnish with strawberries, kiwifruit, avocado and coconut flakes.

TROPICAL SALAD DRESSING

Makes about 2 cups

> 1/2 cup cream of coconut
> 1/3 cup red wine vinegar
> 1 teaspoon dry mustard
> 1 teaspoon salt
> 1 clove garlic
> 1 cup vegetable oil

Combine all the ingredients *except* the oil in a food processor or blender. With machine running, slowly add the oil, blending until smooth. (Store the remaining dressing in the refrigerator and serve with fruit or mixed green salads.)

Mary Caldwell Clark
Nashville, Tennessee

Top to bottom: Tropical Chicken Salad, Turkey-Curry Supper Salad (page 38)

TURKEY-CURRY SUPPER SALAD

♦ Fourth place winner in the "No Small Potatoes" Contest, sponsored by *Family Circle* magazine

Makes 6 servings

5 medium-size red potatoes (about 1½ pounds)
1⅓ cups mayonnaise
1 tablespoon instant minced onion
1 tablespoon curry powder
1 tablespoon white wine vinegar
1 teaspoon celery salt
1 teaspoon paprika
3½ cups diced cooked turkey
1 cup thinly sliced celery
Kale leaves, for serving

Cook the potatoes in 1 inch of boiling salted water in a covered 3-quart saucepan for 30 to 40 minutes or until tender. Drain and cool slightly. Meanwhile, combine the mayonnaise, onion, curry powder, vinegar, celery salt and paprika in a large bowl. Stir in the turkey and celery. Peel and dice the warm potatoes, then fold them into the turkey mixture. Cover and refrigerate for 2 hours or overnight to allow the flavors to blend. Serve the salad on kale leaves.

Mary Franklin
Havre, Montana

Curry powder is formed by blending together a number of spices, including turmeric, cardamom, cumin, pepper, cloves, cinnamon, nutmeg and sometimes ginger. Chilies give it heat and ground dried garlic provides depth of taste. Curry blends vary depending on their use. Milder powders are used for fish and eggs; stronger ones season meats and poultry. There are also regional variations. Store curry powder away from the heat of the stove to preserve its full strength and pungency.

CHICKEN SALAD

♦ First place winner in American Heart's Connecticut Chicken Classic, sponsored by the American Heart Association, Connecticut Affiliate Inc., at the Connecticut Culinary Institute, Farmington, Connecticut

Makes 2 servings

¼ cup broccoli flowerets
6 ounces cubed cooked chicken
½ cup chopped Granny Smith apples
10 seedless red grapes, halved
¼ cup reduced-calorie buttermilk dressing
Red leaf lettuce, for serving (optional)
Parsley, for garnish

If desired, cook the broccoli in boiling water for 3 minutes; drain. Mix broccoli, chicken, apples, grapes and dressing in a medium-sized bowl; toss well. Serve the salad on red leaf lettuce garnished with parsley. Or, serve it as a sandwich using pita pockets or whole grain wheat bread.

William J. Carew
Middlebury, Connecticut

BLUEBERRY ORANGE SALAD

◆ First place winner in the Salads category at the Blueberry Cooking Contest, sponsored by the Bacon County Extension Service, Alma, Georgia

Makes about 12 servings

    2 cups orange juice
    1 (6-ounce) package orange flavor gelatin
1/4 cup sugar
    1 teaspoon grated lemon rind
    2 cups buttermilk
    2 cups fresh blueberries
    Lettuce leaves, for serving

Oil a 6-cup mold. Bring the orange juice to a boil in a large saucepan over medium heat. Remove from the heat and add the gelatin, sugar and lemon rind; stir until the gelatin is dissolved. Refrigerate the mixture until it is the consistency of unbeaten egg whites. Stir in the buttermilk and mix well; fold in the blueberries. Pour into the prepared mold and refrigerate until set. Unmold onto lettuce leaves and serve.

Norma Mims
Alma, Georgia

Unmolding Gelatin Salads

To easily unmold a gelatin salad, follow these steps:

1. Use moistened fingertips to gently pull the gelatin away from the edges of the mold.

2. Dip the mold into a large bowl of warm water for about 10 seconds, immersing it almost to the rim.

3. Cover the mold with a wet serving plate and invert. (The wet plate lets you slide the gelatin to the center.)

4. Give the mold a gentle shake or two. If it does not slide out at once, return it to the bowl of water for a few seconds.

With the exception of iceberg lettuce, all salad greens have a relatively short shelf life and should be eaten as soon as possible. Wash salad greens in plenty of cold water and spin dry in a salad spinner. Or, drain thoroughly and dry with paper towels. If they are not to be eaten immediately, refrigerate them with two or three wet paper towels in a closed plastic bag to keep the leaves crisp.

TOMATO-FILLED ZUCCHINI BOATS

♦ Second place winner in the California Fresh Market Tomato Advisory Board Contest, Los Angeles, California

Makes 8 zucchini boats

   4 medium-size zucchini, each about 6 inches long
 3/4 cup vinaigrette or bottled Italian dressing, divided
   3 large fresh tomatoes, diced
 1/2 cup diced green bell pepper
 1/2 cup diced celery
 1/2 cup diced cucumber
 1/4 cup sliced fresh mushrooms
 1/4 cup chopped ripe olives
   1 clove garlic, very finely chopped
     Salt and freshly ground black pepper to taste
     Salad greens, for serving
     Finely chopped parsley, for garnish

Trim the zucchini; steam or cook in lightly salted simmering water until tender-crisp. Plunge into cold water to stop cooking; drain. Slice each zucchini in half lengthwise and scoop out the seeds. Place the zucchini boats in a shallow dish, cut side up. Drizzle 1/2 cup of the dressing over the boats. Cover and refrigerate for up to 24 hours.

When ready to serve, combine the tomatoes, green pepper, celery, cucumber, mushrooms, olives and garlic with the remaining 1/4 cup dressing. Season with salt and black pepper. Spoon the tomato mixture into the zucchini boats. Arrange the boats on a serving dish lined with salad greens and garnish with parsley.

Selma Goldstein
North Hollywood, California

Carrots have been around since ancient times, but were not widely used until the Middle Ages. At that time, they were red, purple or black in color. It wasn't until the 16th century that a yellow strain became popular. By the next century, in Holland, it had evolved into the familiar orange vegetable we know today.

MARINATED SWEET AND SOUR CARROT SALAD

◆ Third place winner in the Side Dish category at the "Tabletalk" Cooking Contest, sponsored by *The Independence Examiner*, Independence, Missouri

Makes 12 servings

1¹/₂ pounds carrots, thinly sliced
1 medium-size red onion, thinly sliced
¹/₂ cup chopped green bell pepper
1 (10³/₄-ounce) can condensed tomato soup
³/₄ cup sugar
¹/₂ cup vegetable oil
¹/₂ cup red wine vinegar
1 teaspoon Worcestershire sauce (optional)
¹/₂ teaspoon salt

Cook the carrots in boiling salted water in a large saucepan for about 5 minutes or until crisp-tender. Drain and cool. Combine the carrots, onion and green pepper in a serving bowl. Combine the soup, sugar, oil, vinegar, Worcestershire sauce and salt in a small bowl. Pour the marinade over the vegetables and stir gently to combine. Cover and refrigerate for at least 24 hours to blend the flavors. Serve chilled.

Florence Tankersley
Independence, Missouri

French fries have absolutely nothing to do with France. The term is believed to be American in origin and refers to a technique for cutting potatoes into narrow strips, called "frenching."

'TATER-BEAN SALAD

◆ Tenth place winner in the "No Small Potatoes" Contest, sponsored by *Family Circle* magazine

Makes 6 servings

¹/₄ cup Italian dressing
1 (16-ounce) package frozen french fries
1 cup mayonnaise
1 teaspoon salt
1 teaspoon prepared horseradish
1 teaspoon prepared mustard
¹/₈ teaspoon pepper
4 hard-cooked eggs, sliced
1 (16-ounce) can cut green beans, drained
¹/₄ cup chopped onion
Paprika
Diced cooked ham (optional)

Heat the dressing in a large skillet and add the fries. Cook, covered, over low heat for 8 to 10 minutes or until heated through, stirring occasionally. Combine the mayonnaise, salt, horseradish, mustard and pepper in a small bowl; stir into the fries. Add the eggs, beans and onion to the skillet and toss lightly to coat; sprinkle with paprika. For a more substantial salad, add the ham.

Carol Hulka
Muskegon, Michigan

JAPANESE SPROUT SALAD

♦ Prize winner at the Great Harvest Split Pea & Lentil Cook-Off, Moscow, Idaho

Makes 6 servings

  ¹/₄ **cup vegetable oil**
  2 **tablespoons sesame seeds**
  1 **cup rice vinegar**
  ¹/₂ **cup sugar**
  1 **teaspoon salt**
  6 **cups lentil sprouts (sprouts from 1 cup uncooked lentils)***
  4 **carrots, grated**
  4 **seedless cucumbers, unpeeled and cut into matchstick pieces****

Heat the oil in a small skillet. Add the sesame seeds; cook and stir until the seeds are light brown. Remove from the heat and cool. Combine the vinegar, sugar and salt in a small bowl. Stir in the seeds; blend thoroughly. Cover dressing and refrigerate until needed.

Lightly mix the sprouts, carrots and cucumbers in a large bowl; pour the dressing over them. Toss and serve immediately or cover and refrigerate for 1 to 2 hours.

Lentil sprouts are available at health food stores or specialty shops. Or, you can sprout your own; allow about 1 week to grow them. Lentil sprouts can be stored in a plastic bag in the refrigerator up to 7 days.

**If using regular cucumbers, peel and seed them first.*

Janet Murai
Uniontown, Washington

Sprouting Lentils

1. For 1¹/₂ cups of sprouts, place ¹/₄ cup thoroughly rinsed uncooked lentils into a 1-quart glass jar. Fill jar with warm water and soak at room temperature overnight.

2. Cut a square of cheesecloth; place over the top of the jar and secure with a rubber band, jar ring or string. Thoroughly drain off the soaking water by turning the jar upside down.

3. Place the jar on its side and shake it to separate and spread lentils along the side that is downward. Cover jar with a dry cloth towel to protect it from bright sunlight and to let the air circulate.

4. Two or three times a day, rinse the lentils well with lukewarm water; drain thoroughly. Shake the sprouts along the side of the jar and return it to its growing spot. The sprouts are ready when ¹/₂ to 1 inch long. This takes about 1 week.

The size of an olive is no indication of its flavor. Some tiny varieties are bitter while others are quite mild, and the same is true for the large ones. Green olives are harvested before they are fully ripe; black olives have ripened on the tree. Both kinds must be cured in brine before they are fit to eat.

ROTINI SALAD ▶

♦ Fifth place winner in the Sensational Salads Pasta Contest, sponsored by the North Dakota Wheat Commission and North Dakota Mill, Bismarck, North Dakota

Makes 8 to 10 servings

   10 ounces uncooked rotini pasta
    2 to 3 stalks broccoli
    1 (6-ounce) can small pitted ripe olives, drained
   10 to 12 cherry tomatoes, cut in half
   ¹/₂ medium-size red onion, thinly sliced
   ¹/₂ cup Italian salad dressing*
    1 to 2 tablespoons grated Parmesan cheese (optional)
      Freshly ground black pepper to taste

Cook the rotini according to the package directions. Drain; rinse with cold water, then drain again thoroughly. Allow to cool. Meanwhile, remove the flowerets from the broccoli. Peel the stalks and cut into chunks. Cook the broccoli in boiling salted water just until bright green and still crunchy. Drain; rinse with cold water, then drain again thoroughly. Combine the broccoli, rotini, olives, tomatoes, onion and salad dressing in a large bowl. Add the cheese and season with pepper. Cover and refrigerate until chilled.

Use a low-calorie dressing to make a nutritious, low-fat salad.

Diane Amble
Sarles, North Dakota

RAINBOW PASTA SALAD

♦ Fourth place winner in the Sensational Salads Pasta Contest, sponsored by the North Dakota Wheat Commission and North Dakota Mill, Bismarck, North Dakota

Makes 4 servings

    8 ounces uncooked tricolor corkscrew pasta
    2 (4¹/₂-ounce) cans medium-size shrimp, drained *or*
       ¹/₂ pound cooked fresh shrimp
   ¹/₂ cup chopped walnuts (optional)
    2 tablespoons sliced pimiento-stuffed green olives
   ¹/₄ cup French dressing
   ¹/₄ cup mayonnaise
    1 teaspoon very finely chopped onion
      Lettuce leaves, for serving   *(continued)*

Cook the pasta according to the package directions. Drain; rinse with cold water, then drain again thoroughly. Allow to cool. Combine all the ingredients *except* the lettuce leaves in a large bowl and toss to mix well. Cover and refrigerate until chilled. Serve on lettuce leaves.

Jodi Magrum
Braddock, North Dakota

*C*rabmeat obtained from the hard-shell crabs found in abundance in the Chesapeake Bay is one of life's great luxuries. Conveniently available in cans, it will keep in the refrigerator for a few days after opening.

CHESAPEAKE CRAB SALAD

♦ First place winner in the Crab Cooking Contest at the National Hard Crab Derby & Fair, Crisfield, Maryland

Serves 4

   1 cup mayonnaise or salad dressing
   ¼ cup heavy cream, whipped
   ¼ cup chili sauce
   ¼ cup chopped green onions, including green tops
   ¼ cup finely chopped green bell pepper
   1 teaspoon lemon juice
      Salt to taste
   1 large head lettuce
   1 pound crabmeat, picked over to remove traces of
      shell
   2 large tomatoes, cut into wedges
   2 hard-cooked eggs, cut into wedges
      Paprika

Make the dressing by combining the mayonnaise, whipped cream, chili sauce, green onions, green pepper and lemon juice in a small bowl. (There should be about 2 cups of dressing.) Season with salt; cover and refrigerate.

Line 4 large plates with lettuce leaves. Shred the remaining lettuce and arrange on the leaves. Reserve a few large pieces of the crabmeat for a garnish; arrange the remaining chunks on top of the lettuce. Alternate wedges of tomato and hard-cooked egg around the crabmeat. If desired, sprinkle lightly with salt. Pour ¼ cup of the dressing over each salad and sprinkle with paprika. Garnish with the reserved pieces of crabmeat. Pass the remaining dressing.

WARM SCALLOP AND AVOCADO SALAD

♦ Corning Creative Cookery Award at the March of Dimes Gourmet Gala in Monterey, California

Serves 2

2 cups chicken broth, preferably homemade
1/2 pound sea scallops
1/2 cup olive oil
1 1/2 tablespoons sherry wine vinegar
1 teaspoon Dijon-style mustard
    Salt and freshly ground pepper to taste
1/2 pound fresh spinach, steamed and chopped
1 avocado, peeled, seeded, sliced and sprinkled with
    lemon juice
1/3 cup chopped walnuts, toasted

If you buy an avocado that is not fully ripe, put it in a brown paper bag and keep it at room temperature. It will soften within a day or two. When you are ready to eat it, cut it with a stainless steel knife and sprinkle it with lemon or lime juice and this will prevent it from discoloring.

Heat the broth in a medium-sized saucepan over low heat to a simmer; do not allow it to boil. Add the scallops; cover and cook for 2 to 3 minutes or until scallops are opaque and barely cooked. Remove from the heat and pour the scallops and broth into a medium-sized bowl. Place ice in a larger bowl. Set medium-sized bowl into ice so ice comes all the way up its side. Add more ice if necessary. Set aside until you are ready to assemble the salad.

Just before serving, make the dressing. Combine the olive oil, vinegar, mustard, salt and pepper in a small saucepan. Heat to simmering over low heat. Remove the scallops from the broth and slice into thin rounds. Make a bed of spinach on 2 plates. Arrange slices of avocado in a star pattern over the spinach; arrange the scallops in the center of the plate. Sprinkle the walnuts over the top and pour the warm dressing over all.

Anne Anka and Reggie Jackson

POULTRY

Fresh ginger is completely different from dry ginger powder in both appearance and flavor. Resembling a gnarled, tan-colored root, fresh ginger adds its own distinctive pungency and aroma to foods and is used extensively in the dishes of the Far East. Buy it in small quantities and store it, unpeeled, in a covered jar in the refrigerator for two to three weeks.

GINGER SPICY CHICKEN

♦ Grand Prize winner in the Pace® Picante Sauce 40th Anniversary Recipe Contest, sponsored by Pace Foods, Inc.

Makes 4 servings

Salt
2 whole chicken breasts, split, skinned and boned
2 tablespoons vegetable oil
1 medium-size red bell pepper, cut into 2 × 1/4-inch strips (about 1 1/2 cups)
1 medium-size green bell pepper, cut into 2 × 1/4-inch strips (about 1 1/2 cups)
1 (8-ounce can) pineapple chunks in juice, undrained
1/2 cup Pace® Picante Sauce
2 tablespoons chopped cilantro or parsley
2 to 3 teaspoons grated fresh ginger *or* 3/4 to 1 teaspoon ground ginger

Lightly salt the chicken breasts. Heat the oil in a large skillet over medium heat. Add the chicken breasts and cook for about 5 minutes or until lightly browned and cooked through. Remove the chicken and reserve. Add the pepper strips, pineapple, picante sauce, cilantro and ginger to the skillet; cook, stirring frequently, for 5 to 7 minutes or until the peppers are tender and the sauce is thickened. Return the chicken to the skillet and heat through.

Priscilla Yee
Concord, California

Boning a Chicken Breast

1. *For easier handling, freeze the chicken until it is firm, but not hard. Remove the skin.*

2. *For each breast half, use a sharp knife to make three or four arched cuts between the meat and the bone, lifting the meat away with your free hand. (Or, slip your fingers between the meat and the bone and work the meat free without the aid of a knife.)*

3. *When the meat and bone are separated, remove the heavy white tendon that runs along the length of the breast. This will prevent the meat from shrinking as it cooks.*

SAUTÉED CHICKEN BREASTS IN CREAM SAUCE

♦ Winner in the Philly "Hall of Fame" Recipe Contest, sponsored by Philadelphia Brand® Cream Cheese

Makes 4 to 6 servings

  2 whole chicken breasts, split, skinned and boned
  2 tablespoons margarine
1¹/₂ cups thinly sliced mushrooms
  1 cup thinly sliced celery
¹/₂ medium-size onion, thinly sliced
¹/₂ teaspoon pepper
¹/₂ teaspoon dried basil, crushed
¹/₄ teaspoon dried chervil, crushed
¹/₈ teaspoon dried thyme, crushed
¹/₃ to ³/₄ cup dry white wine or sherry, divided
  1 (8-ounce) package cream cheese, cubed
¹/₄ cup milk
2¹/₂ cups (8 ounces) corkscrew pasta, freshly cooked and
      drained
  Chopped parsley, for garnish

Cut the chicken into strips. Melt the margarine in a large skillet over low heat. Add the chicken strips, mushrooms, celery, onion, pepper, basil, chervil and thyme. Cook over medium heat, stirring occasionally, for 10 minutes or until the chicken is tender. Add 2 tablespoons of the wine; reduce the heat and simmer for 5 minutes. Combine the cream cheese and milk in a small saucepan; stir over low heat until smooth. Blend in enough of the remaining wine to make the sauce a pouring consistency. To serve, place the hot pasta on a serving platter. Top with the chicken mixture and pour the cream sauce over all. Sprinkle with the chopped parsley.

Stephen Thomas
Bethlehem, Pennsylvania

*C*ontestants at the Delmarva Chicken Cooking Contest come not only from Delaware, Maryland and Virginia (the vast area that gave the competition its DEL-MAR-VA name), but from all over the country. They are lured by the big prize money and the publicity that always surrounds one of the largest of the food festivals.

OLYMPIC SEOUL CHICKEN

♦ First prize winner in the Delmarva Chicken Cooking Contest, Georgetown, Delaware

Serves 4

   1/4 cup white vinegar
    3 tablespoons soy sauce
    2 tablespoons honey
   1/4 teaspoon ground ginger
    2 tablespoons peanut oil
    8 broiler-fryer chicken thighs, skinned
   10 cloves garlic, coarsely chopped*
    1 teaspoon crushed red pepper
      Hot cooked rice, for serving

Combine the vinegar, soy sauce, honey and ginger in a small bowl and set aside. Heat the oil in a large skillet over medium-high heat. Add the chicken and cook for about 10 minutes or until evenly browned on all sides. Add the garlic and red pepper and cook, stirring, for 2 to 3 minutes. Drain off the excess fat. Add the vinegar mixture. Cover the skillet; reduce the heat and simmer for about 15 minutes or until the chicken is fork-tender. Uncover and cook for about 2 minutes or until the sauce has reduced and thickened. Serve with hot rice.

When cooked, the garlic becomes mellow and is not overpowering.

Muriel Brody
Cumberland, Rhode Island

CHICKEN À LA NANCY

♦ Prize-winning recipe at the March of Dimes Gourmet Gala in Wilmington, Delaware

Serves 2

    2 whole Perdue® chicken breasts, skinned and boned
   1/4 cup vegetable oil
    1 clove garlic, crushed
   1/2 lemon, thinly sliced
   1/2 pound fresh mushrooms, sliced
   1/4 cup dry white wine
    1 tablespoon all-purpose flour
    1 teaspoon salt
   1/4 teaspoon freshly ground pepper
   1/4 teaspoon dried oregano
    1 (14-ounce) can whole artichokes, drained

Pound the chicken breasts to ¼-inch thickness and cut into 2-inch-square chunks. Heat the oil in a large skillet over medium heat. Add the garlic and chicken pieces and cook until the chicken is firm. Remove the chicken from the skillet and add the lemon slices and mushrooms; cook until softened. Return the chicken to the skillet and add the remaining ingredients *except* the artichokes. Cook, stirring frequently, for about 10 minutes or until the chicken is cooked. Add the artichokes to the skillet; heat through and serve. (Do not remove the lemon before serving.)

Frank Perdue

FORTY-CLOVE CHICKEN FILICE

♦ Finalist in the Gilroy Garlic Festival Recipe Contest, Gilroy, California. Courtesy of the Gilroy Garlic Festival Association's *Garlic Lover's Cookbook.*

Makes 4 to 6 servings

1 (3-pound) frying chicken, cut into serving pieces
40 cloves fresh garlic, peeled and left whole
½ cup dry white wine
¼ cup dry vermouth
¼ cup olive oil
4 ribs celery, cut into 1-inch pieces
2 tablespoons finely chopped parsley
2 teaspoons dried basil
1 teaspoon dried oregano
  Pinch of crushed red pepper
1 lemon
  Salt and black pepper to taste

Preheat the oven to 375°F. Place the chicken pieces, skin side up, in a shallow baking pan. Combine the garlic with the wine, vermouth, oil, celery, parsley, basil, oregano and red pepper in a medium-sized bowl and mix thoroughly. Sprinkle the mixture over the chicken pieces. Squeeze the juice from the lemon and pour it over the top. Cut the lemon rind into small pieces and place throughout the pan. Season with salt and black pepper. Cover the pan with aluminum foil and bake for 40 minutes. Remove the foil and bake for another 15 minutes.

Val Filice
Gilroy, California

Peeling Garlic Cloves

The easiest and fastest way to peel garlic cloves is to trim off the ends and crush the cloves with the bottom of a heavy saucepan or the flat side of a large knife. The peels can then be easily removed. If the cloves are to be left whole, trim them and drop into boiling water for 5 to 10 seconds, then place in cold water and drain. The peels should slip right off.

CRANBERRY CHICKEN

♦ American Regional Cuisine Award at the March of Dimes Gourmet Gala in Boston, Massachusetts

Serves 6

    ⅓ cup vegetable oil
     3 cloves garlic, finely chopped
     6 chicken breast halves
       Salt and black pepper to taste
     2 medium-size green bell peppers, sliced into strips
     3 medium-size onions, sliced
    10 large mushrooms, sliced
    ½ cup cider vinegar
     1 (16-ounce) can whole cranberry sauce
     1 cup orange juice
     1 tablespoon cornstarch
     1 tablespoon soy sauce
       Hot cooked rice, for serving
       Orange slices and parsley sprigs, for garnish

Heat the oil in a large skillet over medium-high heat. Add the garlic and chicken breasts and cook until the chicken is browned on all sides. Season with salt and black pepper. Remove the chicken and set aside. Add the green peppers, onions and mushrooms to the pan; cook and stir until the vegetables are softened. Stir in the vinegar, cranberry sauce and orange juice. Add the chicken pieces and cook until the chicken is completely tender. Remove the chicken and keep warm.

Combine the cornstarch and soy sauce with enough water to make a smooth paste. Add this to the sauce and vegetables in the pan. Stir gently over low heat until thickened. Make a bed of hot rice on a serving platter and arrange the chicken pieces over it. (Or, place the chicken in the center of the platter and spoon the rice around it.) Pour the sauce over the chicken and garnish with orange slices and parsley sprigs.

Paul Morse

CHICKEN TIMATAR

♦ Third prize winner in the Delmarva Chicken Cooking Contest, Georgetown, Delaware

Makes 6 servings

4 tablespoons vegetable oil
2 medium-size onions, chopped
6 cloves garlic, very finely chopped
4 whole cardamom pods *or* ¼ teaspoon ground cardamom
1 (1-inch) piece fresh ginger, very finely chopped
1 (1-inch) cinnamon stick
1 teaspoon cumin seeds *or* ¼ teaspoon ground cumin
1 bay leaf
6 whole broiler-fryer chicken legs (thighs attached), skinned
3 medium-size tomatoes, chopped
½ teaspoon salt
½ teaspoon black pepper
⅛ teaspoon ground red pepper
2 tablespoons all-purpose flour
3 tablespoons water

Heat the oil in a large skillet or Dutch oven over medium-high heat. Add the onions, garlic, cardamom, ginger, cinnamon, cumin and bay leaf. Reduce the heat to medium and cook, stirring, for 5 minutes. Add the chicken, tomatoes, salt, black pepper and red pepper. Heat the mixture to boiling, then reduce the heat to low. Cover tightly and simmer for 30 minutes or until the chicken is fork-tender, turning after 15 minutes. Combine the flour and water; stir into the tomato mixture. Cook, stirring, for 5 minutes or until thickened. Remove the cardamom pods, cinnamon stick and bay leaf before serving.

Raymonde F. Woodward
Enosburg East, Vermont

Stir-Frying Techniques

Follow these simple steps for successful stir-frying:

1. Prepare all the ingredients in advance, including cleaning, cutting, measuring and combining.

2. Cut the meat and vegetables into uniform sizes and shapes to ensure even cooking.

3. Make sure the oil is hot before adding any food to the pan. (The best oils to use for stir-frying are peanut oil, corn oil and soybean oil.)

4. Keep the food in constant motion, tossing and stirring it with a flat metal or wooden spatula. This prevents it from burning and also seals in the flavor.

STIR-FRIED CHICKEN

♦ Prize winner at the A-OK Cook-Off, sponsored by various Oklahoma agricultural organizations, Oklahoma City, Oklahoma

Makes about 6 servings

2 large whole chicken breasts, split, skinned and
    boned
2 tablespoons corn oil
2 to 3 ribs celery, thin-sliced diagonally (1 cup)
1 medium-size carrot, sliced diagonally
1 medium-size green bell pepper, cut into thin strips
1 cup sliced mushrooms
1/2 small onion, thinly sliced
1 teaspoon salt
1/4 teaspoon ground ginger
1 (16-ounce) can bean sprouts, drained
1 (5-ounce) can water chestnuts, drained and sliced
1/4 cup water
2 teaspoons cornstarch
2 tablespoons soy sauce
3 cups hot cooked wild rice, for serving
3/4 cup peanuts, for serving

Slice the chicken crosswise into 1/4-inch strips. Heat the oil in a large skillet over high heat. Add the celery, carrot, green pepper, mushrooms, onion, salt and ginger; stir-fry for about 3 minutes or until the vegetables are tender-crisp. Remove them to a warm plate with a slotted spoon and keep warm. Add the chicken strips to the oil in the skillet; stir-fry for 3 to 5 minutes or until the chicken is cooked. Return the vegetables to the skillet and stir in the bean sprouts, water chestnuts and water. Blend the cornstarch with the soy sauce until smooth, then gradually stir the mixture into the hot chicken and vegetables. Cook, stirring constantly, until thickened. Mound the hot wild rice onto a serving platter and spoon the chicken and vegetables over it; sprinkle with the peanuts and serve immediately.

Hope Boyd
McAlester FHA/HERO, Oklahoma

TURKEY CASCADE

♦ Second prize winner at the Oregon Turkey Cook-Off, sponsored by the Oregon Turkey Improvement Association, Salem, Oregon

Makes about 4 servings

 2 teaspoons olive oil
 4 turkey thighs or legs
 1/2 medium-size green bell pepper, diced
 2 green onions, chopped
 1/4 cup water
 1 teaspoon garlic powder
 1/2 teaspoon salt
 1/4 teaspoon ground oregano
 1 tablespoon butter or margarine
 1/4 pound fresh mushrooms, sliced

Today, turkey is no longer restricted to the Thanksgiving table. Because it is low in fat, it is masquerading as everything from bologna to hot dogs to ham. Ground turkey and fresh turkey parts, now available year-round in supermarket meat cases, are finding their way to the dinner table with increasing frequency.

Preheat the oven to 350°F. Heat the oil in a large heavy skillet over medium-high heat. Add the turkey and cook until browned on all sides. Transfer turkey to a baking dish. Add the green pepper, green onions, water, garlic powder, salt and oregano. Cover and bake until the turkey is tender, about 1 to 1 1/2 hours. Melt the butter in a small skillet. Add the mushrooms and cook until tender. Pour the mushrooms over the turkey mixture and stir gently. Bake, uncovered, for 5 more minutes. Cool slightly and serve warm with a vegetable and salad.

Teresa and Gary Bliven
Salem, Oregon

Make a large batch of pesto sauce when fresh summer basil is abundant and freeze it for a variety of uses. Add it to soups, particularly vegetable soups such as minestrone. Combine it with mayonnaise to create a superb dressing for eggs, poultry or even a tuna salad sandwich. Or, toss it with hot pasta for a delectable alternative to tomato sauce.

STUFFED BREAST OF TURKEY WITH PESTO SAUCE

♦ First prize winner at the Oregon Turkey Cook-Off, sponsored by the Oregon Turkey Improvement Association, Salem, Oregon

Makes about 8 servings

    1 (6-pound) turkey breast, split and boned
      Pesto Sauce (recipe follows)
    1 pound sweet Italian sausage, casings removed
1¹/₂ cups chopped fresh mushrooms
  ¹/₄ cup chopped onion
2¹/₂ cups cubed French bread
  ¹/₄ cup toasted pine nuts
    1 egg, beaten
  ¹/₈ teaspoon ground red pepper

Pound each turkey breast half until all one thickness; set aside. Prepare the Pesto Sauce; set aside. Preheat the oven to 350°F. Cook the sausage in a large skillet over medium-high heat until no longer pink. Add the mushrooms and onion; cook and stir over low heat for 5 minutes. Combine the bread, pine nuts, egg, red pepper and 2 tablespoons of the pesto sauce in a large bowl. Add the sausage mixture and mix well.

To stuff the turkey breast, divide the stuffing between the breast halves. Roll up, using wooden toothpicks to seal, as needed. Place in a large baking dish or roasting pan. Spread part of the remaining pesto sauce over the surface of the turkey. Bake, uncovered, for 25 to 30 minutes. Reduce the oven temperature to 325°F. Cover and bake for about 1¹/₂ hours or until turkey is done. Cool slightly, then slice. Spread the remaining pesto sauce over the slices and serve.

PESTO SAUCE

    1 cup packed fresh basil leaves
  ¹/₄ cup packed parsley sprigs
  ¹/₄ cup toasted pine nuts
  ¹/₂ cup olive oil
  ¹/₂ cup grated Parmesan cheese
    3 cloves garlic
  ¹/₈ teaspoon salt
  ¹/₈ teaspoon black pepper

Process all the ingredients in a food processor or blender until well mixed.

Linda Shaw
Salem, Oregon

Cajun Turkey Pockets

♦ Third prize winner at the Oregon Turkey Cook-Off, sponsored by the Oregon Turkey Improvement Association, Salem, Oregon

Makes 6 servings

FILLING
  1 tablespoon margarine
  1/2 cup chopped onion
  1 (14 1/2-ounce) can stewed tomatoes
  2 tablespoons all-purpose flour
  1 1/2 teaspoons hot pepper sauce
  1/2 teaspoon celery salt
  1 1/2 pounds cooked turkey, cubed (about 4 cups)

DOUGH
  4 cups all-purpose flour, divided
  1 tablespoon sugar
  1 teaspoon salt
  2 packages quick-rising yeast
  1 cup water
  1/4 cup milk
  1 tablespoon margarine
  1 egg, beaten

To make the filling, melt the margarine in a large skillet over medium heat. Add the onion and cook until tender. Stir in the tomatoes, 2 tablespoons flour, the pepper sauce and celery salt. Reduce the heat and simmer for 5 to 7 minutes. Stir in the turkey; remove from the heat.

To make the dough, combine 3 cups of the flour, the sugar, salt and yeast in a large bowl. Heat the water, milk and margarine in a small saucepan over low heat until hot (125° to 130°F); stir into the flour mixture. Mix in enough of the remaining flour to make a soft dough. Turn out onto a floured surface and knead for 4 minutes. Roll the dough into an 18 × 12-inch rectangle, then cut into six 6-inch squares.

Preheat the oven to 350°F. Grease a large baking sheet. Divide the turkey filling into 6 equal portions. Place 1 portion in the center of each dough square. Bring the points together over the filling; pinch and twist to seal the points and corners. Place on the prepared baking sheet and cover with a towel. Place the baking sheet over a pan that is half filled with hot water. Let the dough rise for 15 minutes. Brush the pockets with the egg and bake for 25 minutes or until golden brown. Serve hot.

Nancy Miller
Portland, Oregon

TURKEY FAJITAS

♦ Fourth prize winner at the Oregon Turkey Cook-Off, sponsored by the Oregon Turkey Improvement Association, Salem, Oregon

Makes 4 servings

1/2 cup sliced green onions, including green tops
1/2 cup lemon juice
1/2 cup honey
1/2 cup warm water
3 tablespoons vegetable oil
1 clove garlic, very finely chopped
1 (1-pound) package turkey breast slices, cut into
    2 × 3/4-inch strips
1 medium-size yellow or green bell pepper, cut into
    strips
1 medium-size tomato, chopped
1/2 cup chopped cilantro
4 (8-inch) flour tortillas
    Picante sauce, for serving

Combine the green onions, lemon juice, honey and water in a small bowl and set aside. Heat the oil and garlic in a large skillet over medium-high heat. Add the turkey strips and stir-fry for 2 minutes. Add the pepper strips and lemon juice mixture; continue to stir-fry until the liquid has evaporated and the turkey is golden brown. Stir in the tomato and cilantro. Spoon the mixture onto the tortillas. Fold in half or roll up. Serve with picante sauce.

Anne Lesko
Milwaukie, Oregon

A fast-rising favorite of Southwest cooking, fajitas originally referred to slices of fried skirt steak or other inexpensive cuts of meat wrapped in a tortilla. Lately, the word has been used to describe almost anything that is served sizzling hot from the grill, including fish, shrimp, chicken and turkey. Guacamole, fried onions, chilies, shredded lettuce, cilantro, salsa, sour cream and refried beans enhance the fajita experience.

SEAFOOD

Oriental sesame oil is a strong-tasting oil made from sesame seeds. It is used in small amounts for flavoring Oriental foods. Do not substitute it for other oils, such as olive oil. You can buy it in the imported (Oriental) section of the supermarket or in specialty food shops.

SHRIMP WITH CUCUMBER AND RICE

♦ Top honors in the Essence/Uncle Ben's® Good Eating Recipe Contest, sponsored by Uncle Ben's, Inc.

Makes 5 to 6 servings

³/₄ cup dry white wine
1 tablespoon sugar
1 tablespoon cornstarch
3 tablespoons soy sauce
1 pound medium- or large-size raw shrimp, peeled and deveined
2¹/₂ cups water
1 cup Uncle Ben's® Converted Brand Rice
1 tablespoon butter or margarine
1 teaspoon salt (optional)
2 tablespoons Oriental sesame oil
2 cups broccoli flowerets
1 medium-size cucumber, seeded and cut into ¹/₂-inch pieces
1 large red bell pepper, cut into ¹/₂-inch pieces
4 green onions, cut into ¹/₂-inch pieces (optional)
¹/₄ cup toasted sliced almonds, for garnish

Combine the wine, sugar, cornstarch and soy sauce in a medium-sized bowl; mix well. Add the shrimp and let stand, stirring occasionally, while you prepare the rice. Bring the water to a boil in a medium-sized saucepan. Stir in the rice, butter and salt. Cover tightly and simmer for 20 minutes. After the rice has simmered 15 minutes,

(continued)

Top to bottom: Shrimp with Cucumber and Rice, Cantonese Shrimp and Snow Peas (page 68)

heat the oil in a large skillet or wok. Drain the shrimp, reserving the marinade. Add the shrimp to the hot oil; stir-fry for about 3 minutes or until pink. Remove them with a slotted spoon. Add the broccoli, cucumber and red pepper to the skillet and stir-fry for about 3 minutes or until tender-crisp. Add the shrimp and reserved marinade; continue to cook, stirring constantly, for about 2 minutes or until thickened.

After the rice has simmered 20 minutes, stir the green onions into it. Remove from the heat and let stand, covered, for about 5 minutes or until all the water is absorbed. Serve the shrimp mixture over the rice and garnish with the toasted almonds.

Roslyn Campbell
Minot, North Dakota

W̶ith the possible exception of lobster, shrimp are probably the most popular of all shellfish. They range in size from tiny to varieties that are so large that four or five constitute a satisfying dinner. Most people will accept them gladly no matter what their size—as long as they are not overcooked.

CANTONESE SHRIMP AND SNOW PEAS

♦ Prize-winning recipe at the March of Dimes Gourmet Gala in Minneapolis, Minnesota

Makes 6 servings

1¹/₂ **teaspoons Tyler chicken stock base**
　1 cup boiling water
　1 tablespoon vegetable oil
　¹/₂ **cup thinly sliced green onions**
　2 cloves garlic, crushed
1¹/₂ **pounds large frozen raw shrimp, thawed, peeled and deveined**
　1 teaspoon soy sauce
　1 teaspoon honey (optional)
　¹/₂ **teaspoon very finely chopped fresh ginger**
　　Dash of pepper
　9 ounces fresh or frozen snow peas *or* cut green beans
　1 tablespoon cornstarch
　1 tablespoon cold water
　　Whole green onions, for garnish

Dissolve the chicken stock base in the boiling water. Heat the oil in a large skillet over medium-high heat. Add the sliced green onions, garlic and shrimp; cook, stirring frequently, for 3 minutes. If necessary, add a little chicken stock to prevent sticking. Stir in the soy sauce, honey, ginger, pepper, snow peas and the remaining chicken stock. Reduce the heat; cover and simmer for 5 to 7 minutes or until the beans are crisp-tender. Dissolve the cornstarch in the cold water; stir into the skillet and cook, stirring constantly, until thick and clear. Garnish with the whole green onions and serve.

Bobby and Dick Pomerantz

SHRIMP CHARLIE

♦ First prize winner in the Savory category of the International Association of Cooking Professionals Recipe Contest, sponsored by Coco Lopez® Cream of Coconut, a product of Borden, Inc.

Makes 6 to 8 servings

1/2 **cup cream of coconut**
1/2 **cup water**
1 **tablespoon cornstarch**
1/2 **teaspoon salt**
3 **tablespoons vegetable oil**
1 **cup coarsely chopped red or yellow bell pepper**
1/2 **cup coarsely chopped green bell pepper**
1/2 **cup coarsely chopped onion**
2 to 3 **jalapeño peppers, seeded and finely chopped***
 or 3 **tablespoons chopped canned green chilies**
1 **clove garlic, finely chopped**
2 **pounds medium-size raw shrimp, peeled and deveined**
2 **cups seeded and coarsely chopped fresh tomatoes**
 Hot cooked rice, for serving
 Chopped parsley, for garnish

Combine the cream of coconut, water, cornstarch and salt in a small bowl; set aside. Heat the oil in a large skillet over medium-high heat. Add the red and green bell peppers, onion, jalapeños and garlic; cook and stir until tender-crisp. Remove the vegetables with a slotted spoon. Add the shrimp to the oil remaining in the skillet; cook and stir for 1 to 2 minutes or until pink. Add the vegetables and the reserved cream of coconut mixture; cook and stir until slightly thickened. Stir in the tomatoes and heat through. Serve with hot rice and garnish with parsley.

*Wear rubber gloves when working with hot peppers and wash your hands in warm soapy water. Avoid touching your face or eyes.

Patsy Swendson
San Antonio, Texas

𝒫eeling and Deveining Shrimp

Shrimp may be peeled and deveined either before or after they are cooked. If cooked, peel and devein them while they are still warm.

The shell is easily removed with your fingers. Start to peel it off on the side with the legs. Lift it up and over, then back around to the leg side. The tail section may be removed or left intact, depending on how the shrimp are to be used.

To devein shrimp, make a small cut along the back and lift out the dark vein with the tip of a knife. You may find the task easier if it is done under cold running water. There are also special gadgets available that make peeling and deveining shrimp a one-step process.

CHESAPEAKE CRAB STRATA ▶

♦ Grand Prize winner in the Crab Cooking Contest at the National Hard Crab Derby & Fair, Crisfield, Maryland

Makes 6 to 8 servings

4 tablespoons (1/2 stick) butter or margarine
4 cups unseasoned croutons
2 cups (8 ounces) shredded Cheddar cheese
2 cups milk
8 eggs, beaten
1/2 teaspoon dry mustard
1/2 teaspoon Old Bay seasoning
Salt and black pepper to taste
1 pound crabmeat, picked over to remove any shell
Red and green bell pepper rings, for garnish

Preheat the oven to 325°F. Place the butter in an 11 × 7 × 1½-inch baking dish. Heat in the oven until melted, tilting to coat the dish. Remove the dish from the oven; spread the croutons over the melted butter. Top with the cheese and set aside.

Combine the milk, eggs, mustard, Old Bay seasoning, salt and black pepper; mix well. Pour the egg mixture over the cheese in the dish and sprinkle the crabmeat on top. Bake for about 50 minutes or until the mixture is set. Remove from the oven and let stand for about 10 minutes. Garnish with the pepper rings and serve.

Patricia Limber
Crisfield, Maryland

The Crisfield National Hard Crab Derby dates back to 1947 when a few hard-shell crabs were dumped on Main Street and the one that managed to scurry to an outer circle first was declared derby winner. Today, hundreds of crabs compete each Labor Day weekend for the derby trophy, and 50 crabs, representing the 50 states, vie for the Governor's Cup Race trophy. Other events spanning the entire weekend include crab picking and cooking contests, parades and concerts, but the crab derby remains the highlight.

DELMARVA CRAB CAKES ▶

♦ Winner in the Crab Cake category in the Crab Cooking Contest at the National Hard Crab Derby & Fair, Crisfield, Maryland

Makes 4 servings

2 cups crabmeat, picked over to remove any shell
1 cup soft bread crumbs
1/4 cup milk
2 tablespoons mayonnaise
1 tablespoon finely chopped green bell pepper
1 tablespoon lemon juice
1/2 teaspoon salt
4 drops Tabasco pepper sauce
Dash of ground nutmeg
Butter or margarine, for frying
Lemon slices and parsley, for garnish   *(continued)*

Blend all the ingredients *except* the butter, lemon slices and parsley in a medium-sized bowl. Shape the mixture into 8 crab cakes. Melt the butter in an electric skillet set at 350°F. Add the crab cakes and cook for 10 to 20 minutes or until golden brown on each side. Garnish with lemon slices and parsley.

Mrs. James Blizzard
Seaford, Delaware

DEVILED CRAB

♦ Grand Prize winner in the Crab Cooking Contest at the National Hard Crab Derby & Fair, Crisfield, Maryland

Makes 6 servings

    5 tablespoons butter or margarine, divided
 1/2 cup finely chopped onion
 1/4 cup finely chopped green bell pepper
    3 tablespoons all-purpose flour
 1 1/2 cups half-and-half
    2 eggs, beaten
    1 tablespoon finely chopped chives
    1 tablespoon prepared mustard
    2 teaspoons Worcestershire sauce
 1/2 teaspoon salt
      Dash of ground red pepper
    1 pound crabmeat, picked over to remove any shell
    1 cup soft bread crumbs

Preheat the oven to 375°F. Grease 6 ramekins or custard cups or a 1-quart baking dish. Melt 3 tablespoons of the butter in a large saucepan over medium heat. Add the onion and green pepper; cook and stir until tender. Stir in the flour and mix until smooth. Gradually stir in the half-and-half and cook over medium heat, stirring constantly, until the sauce thickens. Gradually stir a small amount of the hot cream sauce into the eggs and combine thoroughly. Stir the egg mixture back into the sauce in the pan and heat gently for 2 minutes. Remove from the heat and add the chives, mustard, Worcestershire sauce, salt and red pepper; mix well. Stir in the crabmeat.

Spoon the crab mixture into the prepared ramekins or casserole. Melt the remaining 2 tablespoons butter in a small skillet. Combine the melted butter with the bread crumbs and sprinkle over the crab mixture. Bake for 20 to 25 minutes or until the crumbs are golden brown. Serve at once.

Nicki Dixon
Crisfield, Maryland

FARM-RAISED CATFISH WITH BACON AND HORSERADISH

♦ First place winner in the National Farm-Raised Catfish Cooking Contest, sponsored by The Catfish Farmers of America, Nashville, Tennessee

Serves 6

   6 (4- to 5-ounce) farm-raised catfish fillets, fresh or
      frozen
   2 tablespoons butter
   1/4 cup chopped onion
   1 (8-ounce) package cream cheese, softened
   1/4 cup dry white wine
   2 tablespoons shredded horseradish
   1 tablespoon Dijon-style mustard
   1/2 teaspoon salt
   1/8 teaspoon pepper
   4 strips bacon, cooked crisp and crumbled
   2 tablespoons finely chopped parsley, for garnish

If frozen, thaw the fish fillets according to the package directions; rinse and pat dry. Preheat the oven to 350°F. Use a little of the butter to grease a large baking dish. Arrange the fillets in a single layer in the dish.

Melt the remaining butter in a small skillet over medium-high heat. Add the onion; cook and stir until softened. Combine the cream cheese, wine, horseradish, mustard, salt and pepper in a small bowl; stir in the onion. Pour this mixture over the fish and top with crumbled bacon. Bake for 30 minutes or until the fish flakes easily when tested with a fork. Serve at once, garnished with parsley.

Marcy Wheeler
Claymont, Delaware

Catfish have become so popular in recent years that their devotees now have their own official fan club! Mild-tasting and adaptable to most cooking methods, farm-raised catfish are most frequently breaded and fried. However, they can also be successfully baked, broiled, poached and even smoked.

FARM-RAISED CATFISH WITH SPINACH AND SOUR CREAM

♦ Third place winner in the National Farm-Raised Catfish Cooking Contest, sponsored by The Catfish Farmers of America, Nashville, Tennessee

Serves 6

 6 (5- to 6-ounce) farm-raised catfish fillets, fresh or frozen
1¼ teaspoons salt, divided
 1 teaspoon black pepper, divided
 2 (10-ounce) packages frozen chopped spinach, thawed and drained
 2 tablespoons grated Parmesan cheese
 6 tablespoons (¾ stick) butter or margarine, divided
 ¼ cup lemon juice
 ¼ teaspoon garlic powder
 ¼ cup chopped green bell pepper
 ¼ cup chopped celery
 ¼ cup finely chopped green onions, including green tops
 2 cups fresh bread crumbs
 ½ cup sour cream
 ½ teaspoon paprika
 Lemon slices and parsley sprigs, for garnish

If frozen, thaw the fish fillets according to the package directions; rinse and pat dry. Sprinkle ¾ teaspoon of the salt and ½ teaspoon of the black pepper over the fillets and set aside. Preheat the oven to 400°F. Lightly grease a 13×9-inch baking dish. Spread the spinach over the bottom of the dish. Sprinkle the remaining ½ teaspoon salt and ½ teaspoon black pepper over the spinach; top with the cheese. Arrange the fillets in a single layer over the spinach. Melt 4 tablespoons of the butter in a small saucepan over medium heat. Stir in the lemon juice and garlic powder. Brush the fillets lightly with the butter mixture; reserve the remaining butter mixture.

Melt the remaining 2 tablespoons butter in a medium-sized skillet over medium heat. Add the green pepper, celery and green onions; stir-fry for 3 minutes. Stir in the bread crumbs and sour cream. Divide this mixture into 6 portions; spread 1 portion over each of the fillets. Pour

(continued)

the reserved butter mixture over all and sprinkle with paprika. Bake for 30 to 35 minutes or until the fish flakes easily when tested with a fork. Garnish with the lemon slices and parsley.

Catherine Kirkland
St. Augustine, Florida

ITALIAN-STYLE FISH AND ▶ *VEGETABLES*

♦ Finalist in the Pillsbury BAKE-OFF® Contest in San Diego, California

Makes 6 servings

>   2 tablespoons olive or vegetable oil
>   1 medium-size onion, sliced
>   1 (2¹/₂-ounce) jar Green Giant® Sliced Mushrooms, drained
>   ¹/₂ teaspoon dried basil
>   ¹/₂ teaspoon fennel seeds
>   2 cups Green Giant® Frozen Mixed Vegetables (from 16-ounce bag)
> 1¹/₂ pounds fresh or frozen catfish, orange roughy or sole fillets, thawed if frozen
>   ¹/₄ teaspoon salt
>   ¹/₄ teaspoon pepper
>   2 medium-size tomatoes, sliced
>   ¹/₃ cup grated Parmesan cheese
>   Fresh basil sprigs, for garnish

Heat the oil in a large skillet over medium heat. Add the onion, mushrooms, basil and fennel seeds; cook for 4 minutes or until the onion is tender. Stir in the frozen mixed vegetables. Place the fish fillets over the vegetables and sprinkle with salt and pepper. Arrange the tomato slices over the fish. Reduce the heat to low; cover and cook for 12 to 16 minutes or until the fish flakes easily when tested with a fork. Remove from the heat and sprinkle with the cheese. Cover and let stand for about 3 minutes or until the cheese is melted. Garnish with basil sprigs, if desired.

Louise Bobzin
Pinellas Park, Florida

Cleaning Shellfish

Even shellfish that is farm raised must be scrubbed carefully to remove all traces of mud and sand before shucking or cooking. Place the shellfish in a large bowl of cold water for a few minutes, then scrub them with a stiff vegetable brush. Repeat this process until they are completely clean, changing the water each time. Lift the shellfish out of the water before immersing them again in cold water. If you drain the shellfish in a colander, don't pour the dirty water over them; place them into the colander first and then discard the soaking water. Be sure to pull out the beardlike growths on mussels and some soft-shell clams.

CIOPPINO

♦ American Regional Cuisine Award winner at the March of Dimes Gourmet Gala in Washington, D.C.

Makes 10 to 12 servings

1 quart mussels, scrubbed and beards removed
3 cups zinfandel or other dry red wine, divided
1/2 cup olive oil
1 large onion, chopped
2 cloves garlic, finely chopped
1 medium-size green bell pepper, chopped
1/2 pound dried mushrooms, soaked and drained
1 (32-ounce) can Italian plum tomatoes, undrained
1/4 cup Italian tomato paste
2 teaspoons salt
1 teaspoon ground black pepper
2 tablespoons finely chopped fresh basil
3 pounds striped bass or other firm fish fillets, cut into bite-sized pieces
1 pound crabmeat, picked over to remove any shell
1 pound medium-size raw shrimp, peeled and deveined
3 tablespoons chopped parsley

Steam the mussels in 1 cup of the wine until open. (Discard any unopened shells.) Strain the mussel liquid through cheesecloth and reserve; leave the mussels in their shells.

Heat the oil in an 8-quart pot. Add the onion, garlic, green pepper and mushrooms; cook and stir for 3 minutes. Add the tomatoes and cook for 4 minutes. Stir in the strained mussel liquid, tomato paste and remaining 2 cups wine. Add the salt and black pepper and simmer for 20 minutes. Taste and correct the seasonings. Add the basil and the fish; cook for about 5 minutes or until the fish flakes easily when tested with a fork. Add the mussels in their shells, crabmeat and shrimp. Heat until the shrimp turn pink. Sprinkle with the parsley and serve.

Ann Landers
Mary Margaret and Jack Valenti

MEATS

eef

LIME-THYME BEEF

♦ Second place winner at the National Beef Cook-Off®, sponsored by the American National CattleWomen, Inc.

Makes 6 to 8 servings

> 1 (3-pound) boneless beef round roast, rolled and tied
> 1/4 cup dry white wine or vermouth
> 1/4 cup vegetable oil
> 3 tablespoons fresh lime juice
> 1 teaspoon dried thyme, crushed
> Orzo with Peas and Pine Nuts (recipe follows)
> 1/2 cup heavy cream
> 2 tablespoons all-purpose flour
> 1/4 teaspoon sugar
> 1/8 teaspoon dill weed
> Salt and pepper to taste
> Lime wedges and cilantro sprigs, for garnish

Pierce the beef all over with a long-tined fork and place in a plastic bag. Combine the wine, oil, lime juice and thyme; pour over the beef. Close the bag securely and marinate in the refrigerator for up to 1 hour, turning occasionally.

Preheat the oven to 350°F. Place the beef and marinade in a roasting pan; cover tightly and cook for 1½ hours or until tender, basting occasionally. Remove the beef and keep warm. Meanwhile, prepare the Orzo with Peas and Pine Nuts. (continued)

*The word orzo
actually means barley,
even though the shape of
this pasta looks more
like rice. It forms a
versatile base for
morsels of cooked meat
and vegetables and is
often used to stuff
tomatoes or peppers.
Look for it in the pasta
section of the grocery
store.*

Strain the pan juices into a saucepan; skim off the fat. Boil the juices until reduced slightly. Combine the cream, flour and sugar; stir into the juices. Cook and stir until thickened. Stir in the dill weed and season with salt and pepper.

Carve the beef into thin slices and arrange on a heated serving platter with the Orzo with Peas and Pine Nuts. Season the meat with salt and pepper, if you wish. Garnish the platter with lime wedges and cilantro. Serve with the sauce on the side.

ORZO WITH PEAS AND PINE NUTS

   4 tablespoons (¹/₂ stick) butter or margarine
¹/₃ cup pine nuts
   8 ounces orzo pasta, cooked and drained
   4 ounces (about 1 cup) frozen peas, cooked and
      drained
   1 small tomato, seeded and chopped (optional)

Melt the butter in a large skillet over medium heat. Add the pine nuts and cook until golden brown. Add the orzo, peas and tomato; heat through and serve.

CHUCK AND APPLES

♦ Third place winner at the National Beef Cook-Off®, sponsored by the American National CattleWomen, Inc.

Makes 6 to 8 servings

   3 pounds boneless beef chuck, well trimmed
¹/₂ cup all-purpose flour
   Salt and pepper to taste
¹/₄ cup vegetable oil
   2 cups apple juice
   1 cup sliced celery
   1 (0.85-ounce) envelope dry onion soup mix
   3 cups sliced apples (about 3 medium-size apples)
   Apple wedges and parsley or watercress sprigs, for
      garnish

Cut the beef into 2-inch cubes. Season the flour with salt and pepper; dredge the beef cubes in seasoned flour. Heat the oil in a large skillet over medium heat. Add the beef and cook until browned. Stir in the apple juice, celery and soup mix. Reduce the heat; cover tightly and simmer for about 1 hour or until the meat is tender, stirring occasionally. Add the sliced apples and continue cooking, covered, for 5 to 7 minutes or until apples are just tender. Transfer the beef and apples to a warm serving platter and garnish with apple wedges and parsley sprigs. Spoon off the fat from the pan juices; serve the juices on the side in a gravy boat.

STUFFED SHELLS CASSEROLE

♦ Fifth place in the "Casseroles of the Century" Pasta Contest, sponsored by the North Dakota Wheat Commission and North Dakota Mill, Bismarck, North Dakota

Makes 4 to 5 servings

1/2 **pound lean ground beef**
20 **uncooked jumbo-sized pasta shells**
 1 **envelope spaghetti sauce seasoning mix** *or* **sloppy
    joe seasoning mix**
 1 **(6-ounce) can tomato paste**
1¼ **cups water**
 1 **(10-ounce) package frozen chopped spinach, thawed
    and squeezed dry**
 1 **cup small curd cottage cheese**
 1 **cup (4 ounces) shredded mozzarella cheese**

Brown the ground beef in a medium-sized saucepan. Drain off and discard the excess fat. Cook the shells according to the package directions until tender, yet firm. Drain; rinse with cold water, then drain again thoroughly.

Preheat the oven to 350°F. Grease an 11 × 7 × 2-inch baking dish. Combine the seasoning mix, tomato paste and water in a small bowl. Add to the ground beef and simmer, covered, over low heat for 20 minutes. Spread half of the meat sauce in the bottom of the prepared dish. Combine the spinach, cottage cheese and mozzarella cheese in a medium-sized bowl; blend thoroughly. Spoon about 2 tablespoonfuls of the cheese mixture into each shell; arrange in the dish, open side up. Spoon the remaining meat sauce over the shells. Cover and bake for 20 minutes or until bubbly.

Minnie Briese
Glasston, North Dakota

Ground beef is a fairly meaningless term. Most people want to know what kind of beef has been ground. To meet USDA standards, all ground beef must be at least 70 percent lean. Ground sirloin and ground round are the leanest. Ground chuck contains more fat and therefore produces juicier hamburgers and meat loaf. If you are not sure what to buy, ask your butcher.

BEEFY MEXICAN CORN BREAD

♦ First runner-up in the Kansas Beef Cook-Off, sponsored by the Kansas CattleWomen and the Kansas Beef Council, Topeka, Kansas

Serves 6

1½ pounds ground beef
 ½ cup vegetable oil
 1 cup yellow cornmeal
 1 teaspoon salt
 ½ teaspoon baking soda
1½ cups milk
 1 (12-ounce) can cream-style corn
 2 eggs, well beaten
 1 large onion, chopped
 2 large green bell peppers, chopped
   Jalapeño peppers, chopped, to taste*
 1 (4-ounce) can green chilies, drained and chopped
 ½ pound cheese (such as Cheddar or Monterey Jack),
   shredded

Preheat the oven to 350°F. Brown the ground beef; drain and discard the excess fat. Remove to paper towels to drain further. Meanwhile, pour the oil into a 10-inch cast-iron skillet and let it heat over low heat. Mix the cornmeal, salt and baking soda in a medium-sized bowl, then stir in the milk and corn. Add the eggs and mix well. Stir in the hot oil from the skillet and mix thoroughly. Pour half of the corn bread batter into the hot skillet. Crumble the ground beef over the top. Layer the onion, green peppers, jalapeño peppers, chilies and cheese over the beef. Cover the top with the remaining corn bread batter. Bake for about 45 minutes. Served with a tossed salad, this makes a complete meal.

Wear rubber gloves when working with hot peppers and wash your hands in warm soapy water. Avoid touching your face or eyes.

Sue Butter
Eureka, Kansas

MEXICAN BEEF PASTIES

Pasties are pastry turnovers filled with meat and vegetables. They originated in Cornwall, England where they have been eaten since the Middle Ages. Pasties were devised to stretch a small amount of meat into a fairly substantial meal. Many countries have their own variations, replacing the pastry with egg roll skins, crêpes, pasta dough or tortillas.

♦ Champion in the Kansas Beef Cook-Off, sponsored by the Kansas CattleWomen and the Kansas Beef Council, Topeka, Kansas

Serves 4

1¹/₂ pounds ground beef
 ³/₄ cup chopped onion
 2 tablespoons chopped green bell pepper
1¹/₂ cups taco sauce
 6 tablespoons ketchup
 2 tablespoons packed brown sugar
 1 teaspoon seasoned pepper
1¹/₂ teaspoons dried oregano
1¹/₂ teaspoons dried basil
 1 teaspoon ground cumin
 ³/₄ teaspoon garlic salt
 2 (9¹/₂-ounce) cans refrigerated pastry pocket dough
   Taco sauce
   Sour cream
   Red, yellow and/or green bell pepper rings, for garnish
   Hot peppers, for garnish

Brown the ground beef with the onion and chopped green pepper in a medium-sized skillet over medium heat, stirring to break the ground beef into pieces. Cook for 8 to 12 minutes or until the onion is tender. Discard the excess fat and add the 1¹/₂ cups taco sauce, the ketchup, sugar and seasonings. Cook over low heat, stirring frequently, for 8 to 10 minutes or until the liquid has nearly evaporated. Remove from the heat and set aside.

Preheat the oven to 375°F. Unroll the dough and separate into 8 squares. Place the dough squares on a large ungreased baking sheet, stretching them slightly. Spoon 6 tablespoons of the reserved filling onto half of each square. Fold the other half of the dough over to cover the filling, forming a rectangular pasty. Press the edges with a fork to seal. Cut three ¹/₂-inch slits in the top of each pasty. Bake for 12 to 15 minutes or until golden brown. Serve the pasties warm. (The filling will be hot.) Top with taco sauce and sour cream; garnish with bell pepper rings and hot peppers.

Barclay J. Brumley
Manhattan, Kansas

SPINACH LASAGNA

♦ First place in the "Casseroles of the Century" Pasta Contest, sponsored by the North Dakota Wheat Commission and North Dakota Mill, Bismarck, North Dakota

Makes 8 to 10 servings

8 ounces uncooked lasagna noodles
1 pound lean ground beef
2 (15½-ounce) jars spaghetti sauce
¼ cup chopped onion
1 (6-ounce) can tomato paste
1 (4-ounce) can mushroom stems and pieces, drained
½ teaspoon parsley flakes
½ teaspoon dried oregano
½ teaspoon dried basil
¼ teaspoon garlic powder
   Seasoned salt and pepper to taste
1 pound dry curd cottage cheese
3 cups (12 ounces) shredded mozzarella cheese, divided
3 ounces grated Romano cheese
1 egg, lightly beaten
1 (10-ounce) package frozen chopped spinach, thawed and well drained
½ cup grated Parmesan cheese
3 ounces sliced pepperoni (optional)*

Mozzarella is a soft white cheese that melts easily. In southern Italy, where it originated, it is made from the milk of buffaloes. In other parts of Italy and in North America, it is made from cows' milk.

Preheat the oven to 350°F. Cook the lasagna noodles according to the package directions. Drain; rinse with cold water, then drain again thoroughly. Brown the ground beef in a large skillet over medium heat. Drain off and discard the excess fat. Add the spaghetti sauce, onion, tomato paste, mushrooms and seasonings. Cook and stir until the mixture comes to a boil. Remove from the heat and set aside.

Combine the cottage cheese, 1 cup of the mozzarella cheese, the Romano cheese, egg and spinach in a medium-sized bowl. Spoon 1½ cups of the meat sauce into a 13 × 9 × 2-inch pan. Add a layer of lasagna noodles, then 1½ to 2 cups of the cheese mixture. Sprinkle with

(continued)

If you use the pepperoni, arrange the slices in a middle layer of the lasagna. Precooking it, either in the microwave or in a skillet, and draining it on paper towels will eliminate some of the grease.

the Parmesan cheese. Repeat the layers using the remaining sauce, noodles and cheese mixture. Top with the remaining 2 cups mozzarella cheese. Bake for 30 to 45 minutes or until bubbly. Place under the broiler for a few minutes to brown the cheese. Let the lasagna stand 10 minutes before serving.

Beverly Grimsley
Fargo, North Dakota

LIPTON® STUFFED CABBAGE ▶ ROLLS

♦ Third place winner in the Senior High category in the "Cook America's Heritage" Recipe Contest, sponsored by Scholastic, Inc. and Lipton® Recipe Soup Mix

Makes 20 rolls

  1 medium-size head cabbage
  1 (32-ounce) jar prepared spaghetti sauce
  1 pound ground beef
  3 cups cooked white rice
  **1 envelope Lipton® Onion-Mushroom Recipe
      Soup Mix**
  1/2 teaspoon salt
  1/4 teaspoon pepper

Preheat the oven to 350°F. Remove the core from the cabbage, then remove the 20 largest leaves. Bring water to a boil in a large saucepan; add the cabbage leaves and cook for 3 minutes or until tender. Drain and set aside.

Pour the spaghetti sauce into a 13 × 9 × 2-inch baking dish and set aside. Brown the ground beef in a medium-sized skillet; drain off and discard the excess fat. Combine the ground beef, rice, soup mix, salt and pepper. Place 3 tablespoons of the beef mixture at one end of each cabbage leaf. Tuck the sides of the leaf over the filling and roll up. Secure the rolls with wooden toothpicks. Place the stuffed cabbage rolls in the prepared dish. Cover and bake for 1 hour. Remove the toothpicks before serving.

Tracy Domigan
Pelham High School
Pelham, New Hampshire

Making a
Lemon Peel Rose

Using a vegetable peeler, remove a long, wide strip of peel from around a lemon, being careful not to remove any of the white pith. Wind up the strip to form a rose shape. Remove a second strip of peel from the lemon, shorter and narrower than the first. Wind up and place it inside the other strip to form the center of the rose.

BEEF FILLETS SUPREME

♦ Second prize winner in the Indoor category at the National Beef Cook-Off®, sponsored by the American National CattleWomen, Inc.

Makes 6 servings

    1 teaspoon lemon pepper
    ½ teaspoon ground cardamom
    6 (4-ounce) beef tenderloin steaks, cut 1 inch thick
    3 tablespoons butter
    8 small mushrooms, thinly sliced
    2 tablespoons diagonally sliced green onions (½ inch thick)
    2 tablespoons white wine
    1 tablespoon light soy sauce
    1 teaspoon Dijon-style mustard
      Lemon peel rose, for garnish
      Green onions, for garnish
      Citrus leaves, for garnish

Combine the lemon pepper and cardamom and sprinkle over the tenderloin steaks. Heat the butter in a large heavy skillet over medium heat until bubbling; do not allow it to burn. Add the steaks and panfry for 7 to 8 minutes or to desired doneness, turning once. Remove the steaks to a heated platter and keep warm. Add the mushrooms and sliced green onions to the skillet and stir-fry for 2 to 3 minutes. Stir in the wine, soy sauce and mustard, scraping up any brown bits sticking to the skillet; heat thoroughly. Pour the sauce over the steaks and garnish with lemon peel rose, green onions and citrus leaves.

Bette Dryer
Indianola, Iowa

arinating less tender cuts of meat in a bath of oil, vinegar and herbs provides a twofold benefit: it infuses the meat with a wonderful flavor and also penetrates the meat fibers to help tenderize them. Place the meat in a plastic bag or shallow glass or stainless steel container. Pour the marinade over the meat, cover and refrigerate for a few minutes, hours or days, depending on the tenderness of the cut. Turn the meat occasionally so the marinade penetrates evenly. Fish, poultry and even vegetables may also be marinated to add extra flavor.

TROPICAL GRILLED FLANK STEAK WITH FRUIT SALSA

♦ First prize winner in the Outdoor category at the National Beef Cook-Off®, sponsored by the American National CattleWomen, Inc.

Makes 4 servings

1/4 cup fresh orange juice
2 tablespoons chili sauce
2 tablespoons soy sauce
2 tablespoons vegetable oil
1 teaspoon sugar
1 teaspoon grated orange rind
2 cloves garlic, very finely chopped
1/2 teaspoon salt
1/8 teaspoon hot pepper sauce
1 beef flank steak (about 1½ pounds)
1 medium-size orange, thinly sliced
    Fruit Salsa (recipe follows)
    Orange wedges, for garnish
    Cilantro sprigs, for garnish

Combine the orange juice, chili sauce, soy sauce, oil, sugar, orange rind, garlic, salt and hot pepper sauce in a small bowl. Place the flank steak in a plastic bag; add the orange juice mixture, turning to coat the steak. Place the orange slices on top of the steak. Close the bag securely and marinate in the refrigerator for 3 hours or overnight, turning occasionally. Pour off the marinade and orange slices and discard.

Light a charcoal grill and begin cooking when the coals reach medium heat.* Place the steak on the grid and grill for 10 to 14 minutes or to desired degree of doneness, turning once. Meanwhile, prepare the Fruit Salsa. Carve the steak across the grain into thin slices. Serve with the salsa and garnish with orange wedges and cilantro.

(continued)

*Coals have reached medium heat when you can **cautiously** hold the palm of your hand 4 inches above the coals for a count of 4 seconds.*

FRUIT SALSA

Makes about 2¹/₂ cups

¹/₂ cup diced pineapple
¹/₂ cup diced mango
¹/₂ cup diced papaya
¹/₂ cup diced green apple
¹/₄ cup diced red bell pepper
¹/₄ cup diced green bell pepper
  2 tablespoons rice vinegar or white wine vinegar
  1 tablespoon finely chopped cilantro
  4 teaspoons sugar
¹/₄ teaspoon crushed red pepper

Combine all the ingredients. Cover and refrigerate before serving. (If you wish, the salsa may be prepared 1 day in advance.)

Debbie Vanni
Libertyville, Illinois

FRANKLY FLANK

♦ Second place winner in the Indiana Beef Cook-Off Contest, sponsored by the Indiana Beef Council, Indianapolis, Indiana

Serves 4 to 6

  1 small onion, chopped
  1 teaspoon salt
¹/₂ teaspoon pepper
  1 cup Worcestershire sauce
  2 tablespoons grated horseradish
  1 teaspoon garlic powder
  1 (28-ounce) bottle ketchup
  1 (2-pound) flank steak
    Lettuce leaves and peach halves, for garnish

Combine the onion, salt, pepper, Worcestershire sauce, horseradish, garlic powder and ketchup in a large bowl; mix thoroughly. Add the flank steak, turning to coat. Cover and marinate in the refrigerator overnight.

When ready to cook, preheat the oven to 350°F. Remove the steak from the marinade; reserve the marinade. Wrap the steak in foil and place it in a baking dish. Bake for 45 minutes. A few minutes before the steak is done, heat the marinade to a boil in a small saucepan; boil for 1

The Hindu recipe for Worcestershire sauce was brought to England by Sir Marcus Sandys, a former governor of Bengal. Having eaten the sauce for many years, he was anxious to share it with his friends and have a supply for himself. He took the recipe to a drugstore in Worcestershire, and there the shop owners, Mr. John Lea and Mr. William Perrins, not only recreated the sauce, but soon expanded into larger quarters as the popularity of their condiment spread around the world.

minute. Remove the foil from the steak and pour the hot marinade over the meat. Return to the oven briefly to let the juices blend. Serve the steak on a platter garnished with lettuce leaves and peach halves. Stir the sauce remaining in the baking dish thoroughly and pour it into a warm gravy boat.

Norma Mehringer
Martinsville, Indiana

KOREAN BEEF

♦ Third place winner in the Junior High category in the "Cook America's Heritage" Recipe Contest, sponsored by Scholastic, Inc. and Lipton® Recipe Soup Mix

Makes about 4 servings

   1 envelope Lipton® Beefy Onion Recipe Soup Mix
3/4 cup water
   3 medium-size cloves garlic, finely chopped
   3 tablespoons sugar
   3 tablespoons vegetable oil
   3 tablespoons soy sauce
   2 pounds boneless beef sirloin steak, cut into 1-inch
      pieces
      Hot cooked rice, for serving

Combine the soup mix, water, garlic, sugar, oil and soy sauce in a medium-sized bowl until thoroughly blended. Add the beef; cover and marinate in the refrigerator overnight.

In an electric skillet set at 375°F, cook the beef with the marinade for 8 minutes or until the beef is done. Remove the beef and keep warm. Cook the marinade an additional 2 minutes or until thickened. To serve, arrange the beef and marinade over hot rice.

Carly Kelly
Christian School of York
Wellsville, Pennsylvania

Pork

RHUBARB PORK LOIN

♦ Fourth place winner in the Good Ideas with Boneless Pork Recipe Contest, sponsored by the National Pork Producers Council

Serves about 6

1 (3-pound) boneless pork loin roast, rolled
1 clove garlic, cut into 8 to 10 slivers
1 teaspoon dried rosemary, crushed
4 stalks rhubarb, sliced (about 2 cups)
1/4 cup plus 2 tablespoons honey
1/4 cup cider vinegar
6 whole cloves
1/2 teaspoon salt
1/2 teaspoon dry mustard
2 to 3 drops red food coloring (optional)

Preheat the oven to 350°F. Place the pork roast in a roasting pan. Cut 8 to 10 slits in the surface of the pork and insert the slivers of garlic. Rub the entire surface of the roast with rosemary. Insert a meat thermometer so the bulb is centered in the thickest part, not resting in fat. Roast the pork for about 1 hour.

Meanwhile, combine the remaining ingredients in a small heavy saucepan. Bring to a boil; reduce the heat and simmer for about 10 minutes. Pour the rhubarb sauce over the pork and continue to roast, basting often, for about 45 minutes or until the pork reaches an internal temperature of 155°F. Remove the pork roast from the oven and let it stand for 10 minutes to allow the internal temperature to rise to 160°F. Carve the roast into thin slices. Heat the rhubarb sauce remaining in the pan and serve with the pork. Garnish as desired.

Nancy Korondan
Aurora, Illinois

Rhubarb is also known as "pieplant" because it is frequently teamed with strawberries and used as a filling for pies. Its long pink or red stalks are very tart and must be sweetened with a generous dose of honey or sugar. When cooking rhubarb into a sauce, take care not to overcook it and add only a small amount of water to the pan. Too much cooking or water will turn it into mush. Always discard the rhubarb leaves; they contain oxalic acid and are toxic.

Pork tenderloin is exactly what it sounds like: the most tender cut of meat from the loin. It is a strip of meat that lies along each side of the backbone. When it is cut crosswise into slices, it forms circles that are called medallions. Often recipes call for the medallions to be pressed so they smooth out and cook more evenly. To do this, simply press down on the medallion with the flat side of a large knife, a meat pounder or the heel of your hand.

PORK TENDERLOIN DIANE ▶

♦ Grand Prize winner in the Good Ideas with Boneless Pork Recipe Contest, sponsored by the National Pork Producers Council

Serves 4

> 1 pound pork tenderloin, cut crosswise into 8 pieces
> 2 teaspoons lemon pepper
> 2 tablespoons butter
> 2 tablespoons lemon juice
> 1 tablespoon Worcestershire sauce
> 1 teaspoon Dijon-style mustard
> 1 tablespoon finely chopped chives or parsley
> Whole chives, for garnish

Press out each tenderloin piece into a 1-inch-thick medallion; sprinkle the surfaces with lemon pepper. Melt the butter in a large heavy skillet over medium heat. Add the medallions and cook for 3 to 4 minutes on each side. Remove the pork to a serving platter and keep warm. Add the lemon juice, Worcestershire sauce and mustard to the pan juices in the skillet. Cook, stirring, until heated through. Pour the sauce over the medallions; sprinkle with the chopped chives. Garnish with the whole chives.

Janice Elder
Spartanburg, South Carolina

WEST INDIAN PORK

♦ Third place winner in the Good Ideas with Boneless Pork Recipe Contest, sponsored by the National Pork Producers Council

Serves 4

> 1 pound pork tenderloin, cut crosswise into 1-inch pieces
> 4 tablespoons ($1/2$ stick) butter, divided
> 2 medium-size bananas, peeled and sliced
> $1/4$ cup packed brown sugar
> $1/4$ cup brandy or rum

(continued)

Flatten the pork tenderloin pieces slightly with the heel of your hand. Melt 1 tablespoon of the butter in a large skillet over medium heat. Add the pork and cook quickly for 4 to 5 minutes or until browned on both sides. Remove the pork from the skillet and keep warm.

Melt the remaining 3 tablespoons butter in the same pan. Add the bananas and cook for 2 to 3 minutes. Add the brown sugar and brandy; cook and stir until the sauce is thick and bubbly. Return the pork to the pan; cook just until heated through. Serve immediately.

Chris Ryder
Cameron Park, California

SOUTHWESTERN STIR-FRY ▶

♦ First place winner in the Good Ideas with Boneless Pork Recipe Contest, sponsored by the National Pork Producers Council

Serves 4

    1 pound pork tenderloin
    2 tablespoons dry sherry
    2 teaspoons cornstarch
    1 teaspoon ground cumin
    1 clove garlic, finely chopped
  1/2 teaspoon seasoned salt
    1 tablespoon vegetable oil
    1 medium-size onion, thinly sliced
    1 medium-size green bell pepper, cut into strips
  12 cherry tomatoes, halved
       Warm flour tortillas and green chili salsa, for
         serving

Cut the pork tenderloin lengthwise into quarters. Cut the quarters into 1/4-inch-thick slices. Combine the sherry, cornstarch, cumin, garlic and seasoned salt in a medium-sized bowl. Add the pork slices and stir to coat. Heat the oil in a large heavy skillet over medium-high heat. Add the pork mixture and stir-fry for 3 to 4 minutes. Stir in the onion, green pepper and tomatoes. Reduce the heat; cover and simmer for 3 to 4 minutes. Serve hot with tortillas and salsa.

Priscilla Yee
Concord, California

*W*hether it hails from Hampshire, Kentucky, Virginia, Westphalia or Bavaria, ham actually comes from the hind leg of a pig. It is usually thought of as a cured meat, although it can be purchased uncured and is then referred to as fresh ham or pork leg. The distinctive flavors of hams are produced by the pigs' diets—peanuts, acorns, apples, corn or peaches—and the type of wood over which they are smoked—apple, hickory or oak.

GRANNY SMITH'S PORK ▸

♦ Winner in the "New Favorites with Fresh Ham" category in the Good Ideas with Boneless Pork Recipe Contest, sponsored by the National Pork Producers Council

Serves about 4

  2 tablespoons vegetable oil
  1 pound boneless pork leg, cut into 1/2-inch cubes
  4 Granny Smith or other tart cooking apples, cored
      and cut into 1/2-inch wedges
  1 cup dry white wine or chicken broth, divided
  1/2 cup packed brown sugar
  1/4 cup cider vinegar
  3 tablespoons cornstarch
  2 tablespoons Worcestershire sauce
  1/2 teaspoon salt
  1/4 teaspoon pepper
      Hot cooked noodles or rice, for serving

Heat the oil in a large skillet over medium heat. Add the pork and brown on all sides. Add the apple slices and cook for 3 minutes, stirring occasionally. Add 1/2 cup of the wine. Reduce the heat; cover and simmer for 10 minutes. Mix the remaining 1/2 cup wine with the remaining ingredients *except* the noodles and add to the skillet. Cook over medium heat, stirring constantly, until the sauce thickens. Serve over hot noodles.

Suzanne Osterstrom
Taylor, Pennsylvania

BERRY SPECIAL PORK CHOPS ▸

♦ Fourth place winner in the Good Ideas with Boneless Pork Recipe Contest, sponsored by the National Pork Producers Council

Serves 4

  3/4 cup fresh cranberries
  1/4 cup orange marmalade
  1/4 teaspoon ground cloves
  4 boneless pork loin chops, cut 3/4 inch thick (about
      1 pound)
  4 tablespoons honey

(continued)

*P*ot pies are among the glories of country cooking. American in origin, they consist of chunks of cooked meat and vegetables enveloped in a sauce, placed in a deep dish or pie pan and covered with a blanket of flaky pastry. The term pot pie first appeared in American print as early as 1792.

*S*ince 1970 the people of Athens, Texas, have staged the Black-Eyed Pea Jamboree. It's a wildly popular annual celebration that draws crowds of people to join in the fun and games and beat their feet to the sounds of country music. The high point is the judging of the reci-peas, and the winners agree to cook up enough of their concoctions to feed 500 people. Imagine the scene when a winner once produced a Pea-tini, which was (you guessed it) a martini sporting a black-eyed pea on a toothpick!

Preheat the oven to 325°F. Thoroughly grease a roasting pan. Coarsely crush the cranberries; mix with the marmalade and cloves. Cut a deep pocket in one side of each pork chop; fill the pockets with the marmalade mixture. Place the chops in the prepared pan and spoon 1 tablespoon of honey over each one. Bake for 45 minutes or until the chops are nicely glazed. Garnish as desired.

Jean Jamieson
Daly City, California

GRANNY'S PEA POT PIE

♦ Grand Champion/First place recipe at the Black-Eyed Pea Jamboree, Athens, Texas

Makes 1 (9-inch) pot pie

   3 tablespoons butter
   1 pound fresh mushrooms, chopped
   1 cup finely chopped onion
   2 tablespoons all-purpose flour
   1/2 teaspoon salt
   1/2 teaspoon garlic salt
   1/4 teaspoon dried thyme
   1/8 teaspoon pepper
   3 cups cooked black-eyed peas, chopped
   1/4 cup sour cream
   1 pound sausage, cooked and crumbled
   3/4 cup (3 ounces) shredded Cheddar cheese
   2 tablespoons chopped pimiento
   2 (9-inch) refrigerated pie crusts

Preheat the oven to 400°F. Melt the butter in a large skillet over low heat. Add the mushrooms and onion and cook until tender. Add the flour, salt, garlic salt, thyme and pepper; mix well. Stir in the black-eyed peas, sour cream and sausage. Cook over low heat until the mixture thickens; *do not boil*. Stir in the cheese and pimiento; remove from the heat and set aside.

Line a 9-inch pie plate with one of the pie crusts and fill with the pea mixture. Top with the second pie crust and seal the edges. Cut slits in the top shell and bake for 12 to 15 minutes or until golden brown.

Bertha Anne Hatton
Murchison, Texas

POLISH REUBEN CASSEROLE

♦ Third place in "Casseroles of the Century" Pasta Contest, sponsored by the North Dakota Wheat Commission and North Dakota Mill, Bismarck, North Dakota

Makes 8 to 10 servings

>   2 (10³/₄-ounce) cans condensed cream of mushroom
>   soup
> 1¹/₃ cups milk
>   1 tablespoon prepared mustard
> ¹/₂ cup chopped onion
>   2 (16-ounce) cans sauerkraut, rinsed and drained
>   1 (8-ounce) package uncooked medium-width noodles
> 1¹/₂ pounds Polish sausage, cut into ¹/₂-inch pieces
>   2 cups (8 ounces) shredded Swiss cheese
> ³/₄ cup whole wheat bread crumbs
>   2 tablespoons butter, melted

Preheat the oven to 350°F. Grease a 13 × 9 × 2-inch baking dish. Mix the soup, milk, mustard and onion in a medium-sized bowl until thoroughly blended. Spread the sauerkraut in the prepared dish. Top with the uncooked noodles. Spoon the soup mixture evenly over the noodles. Top with the sausage, then the cheese. Combine the crumbs and butter. Sprinkle the crumbs over the cheese. Cover the dish tightly with foil; bake for 1 hour or until the noodles are tender.

Darlene Lutz
New England, North Dakota

Polish sausage is also called kielbasa. It is garlicky flavored and consists mainly of seasoned pork, although beef and veal are often added. It is commonly sold in long links that are smoked and precooked, ready to heat and serve. The method for making kielbasa has remained virtually unchanged for more than five hundred years and sausage connoisseurs consider it perfection.

SUNSHINE CASSEROLE

♦ Second place winner in the All American Recipe Contest, sponsored by Ore-Ida® Potatoes

Makes 8 servings

>   1 (20-ounce) package frozen Ore-Ida® Hash Browns
> ¹/₂ pound sausage links, cooked and cut into ¹/₂-inch
>   slices
> 1¹/₂ cups (6 ounces) shredded Monterey Jack or Cheddar
>   cheese
>   6 eggs, lightly beaten
>   4 cups milk
>   1 tablespoon finely chopped onion
>   1 teaspoon Dijon-style mustard
>   Paprika
>   1 medium-size tomato, sliced, for garnish

(continued)

Grease a 13 × 9-inch baking pan. Cook the hash browns according to the package directions. Spread them in a single layer in the prepared pan. Spread the sausage and cheese evenly over the potatoes. Combine the eggs, milk, onion and mustard in a large bowl and pour the mixture over the top. Sprinkle with the paprika. Cover and refrigerate for at least 1 hour or overnight.

When ready to cook, heat the oven to 325°F. Bake the casserole, uncovered, for about 1 hour or until a knife inserted into the center comes out clean. Let stand for 10 to 15 minutes. Garnish with tomato slices and serve.

Annabelle Day
Columbia Public Schools
Columbia, Missouri

CALIFORNIA LAYERED POTATO ▸ SHOWCASE

♦ Second place winner in the "No Small Potatoes" Contest, sponsored by *Family Circle* magazine

Makes 6 to 8 servings

   1 cup small curd cottage cheese
   1 egg
   6 medium-size russet potatoes (about 2 pounds), cooked, peeled and shredded
   2 cups (about 10 ounces) diced cooked ham
   2 cups (8 ounces) shredded Monterey Jack cheese with jalapeño peppers
   1 (16-ounce) package frozen chopped broccoli
   1 (4-ounce) can chopped ripe olives, drained
  1/2 cup chopped red bell pepper or pimiento, for garnish

Preheat the oven to 350°F. Combine the cottage cheese and egg in a large bowl. Add the potatoes and toss to mix. Press the potato mixture into the bottom of an ungreased 3-quart glass baking dish. Sprinkle the ham, cheese and broccoli over the potato mixture. Arrange the olives in 4 diagonal rows over the top. Bake for 45 minutes or until thoroughly heated. Garnish with chopped red pepper placed diagonally between the rows of olives.

Nan Kiefer
San Diego, California

*L*amb

LAMB RIBLETS BARBECUED

*L*amb riblets or spareribs come from the breast portion of the lamb, not the rib portion. The lamb breast is cut between the ribs to form riblets. They are best braised, or marinated and grilled. Allow about two servings per pound of riblets.

♦ Prize-winning recipe at the Natrona County Woolgrowers Lamb Cook-Off, Natrona County, Wyoming

Makes about 6 servings

1 (15-ounce) can tomato sauce
1 cup red wine vinegar
1 cup red wine
1/2 cup olive oil
1/2 cup packed brown sugar
1/4 cup dry mustard
3 tablespoons Worcestershire sauce
3 tablespoons steak sauce
1 teaspoon Tabasco pepper sauce
   Garlic salt or garlic cloves to taste
   Salt and black pepper to taste
3 to 4 pounds lamb riblets

Thoroughly combine all the ingredients *except* the riblets in a medium-sized bowl. Place the riblets in a shallow baking dish; pour the sauce mixture over them. Cover and marinate in the refrigerator for at least 4 hours, turning often.

Preheat the oven to 300°F. Bake the ribs for about 1½ hours or until tender. (Or, grill them, basting frequently, for 20 to 25 minutes.)

Charles Bason
Casper, Wyoming

Top to bottom: Lamb Riblets Barbecued,
Lamb Kebobs (page 113)

BUSH PILOT STEW WITH DUMPLINGS

♦ Prize-winning recipe at the Sheepherders Fair and Lamb/ Mutton Stew Cook-Off, Powder River, Wyoming

Makes 10 to 12 servings

1/2 cup all-purpose flour
2 teaspoons salt
1/2 teaspoon pepper
3 pounds mutton or lamb, cut into cubes
2 tablespoons butter
1 tablespoon vegetable oil
1/2 cup sliced green onion or celery tops
2 tablespoons finely chopped parsley
1 teaspoon dried thyme
1/2 teaspoon ground allspice
1 bay leaf
2 cloves garlic, chopped, *or* 1 teaspoon garlic powder
4 cups water
1 pound small onions
1 pound baby carrots
1 pound small new potatoes
1 pound cauliflower, separated into flowerets
1 pound broccoli, separated into flowerets
    Dumplings (recipe follows)
3 tablespoons all-purpose flour
1/4 cup warm water
    Finely chopped parsley, for garnish

Combine the 1/2 cup flour, the salt and pepper in a small bowl. Dredge the lamb in this mixture, shaking off any excess. Heat the butter and oil in an 8-quart Dutch oven. Add the floured meat and cook until browned. Stir in the onion tops, 2 tablespoons parsley, thyme, allspice, bay leaf and garlic; add the 4 cups water. Bring to a boil, then reduce the heat. Cover and simmer for 30 minutes, stirring occasionally. Add the onions, carrots and potatoes. Cover and simmer over low heat for 30 minutes. Do not boil. Add the cauliflower and broccoli flowerets and simmer, covered, for another 20 minutes. Meanwhile, prepare the Dumplings.

Combine the 3 tablespoons flour with the 1/4 cup warm water; mix well, stirring until smooth. Stir this mixture into the stew and cook until the liquid is thickened. Remove and discard the bay leaf. Drop the dumpling mixture by tablespoonfuls onto the stew and cook,

(continued)

uncovered, over low heat for 10 minutes. Cover and continue cooking for about 10 minutes or until the dumplings are done. Garnish with chopped parsley.

DUMPLINGS

2 cups biscuit baking mix
1/2 cup milk
1 egg, lightly beaten
2 tablespoons finely chopped parsley
1 teaspoon dried tarragon

Combine the biscuit mix, milk, egg, parsley and tarragon in a small bowl. Stir just until the ingredients are moistened and mixed. Set aside.

Tom Hutchison

*B*utterflying a Leg of Lamb

A butterflied leg of lamb is a boned leg that is cut almost in half, then spread open. It is particularly suited to broiling and grilling. Usually the butcher will butterfly the boned leg for you. If you prefer to do it yourself, follow these instructions:

Place the boneless leg fat side down. Cut horizontally through the thickest portions, stopping about 1 inch from the opposite edge so that the meat can open like a book—it should be oval in shape and have a uniform thickness. Lightly pound the opened meat and remove any fat thicker than 1/4 inch.

MARINATED LEG OF LAMB

♦ First place winner at the High Country Lamb Cook-Off, Greeley, Colorado

Serves 8

1 (12-ounce) can beer
1/2 cup sliced green onions
3 tablespoons soy sauce
1/4 teaspoon ground red pepper
1/2 cup chopped green bell pepper
1 tablespoon sugar
2 cloves garlic, very finely chopped
1 (4-pound) leg of lamb, boned and butterflied
   Horseradish sauce, for serving

Combine the beer, green onions, soy sauce, ground red pepper, green pepper, sugar and garlic in a small bowl. Place the lamb in a large baking dish and pour the marinade over it. Cover and marinate in the refrigerator for 6 to 8 hours or overnight, turning occasionally.

Light a charcoal grill and begin cooking when the coals reach medium heat.* Place the lamb on the grid and grill for about 25 minutes on each side or until medium-rare. Serve with horseradish sauce.

*Coals have reached medium heat when you can **cautiously** hold the palm of your hand 4 inches above the coals for a count of 4 seconds.*

ABC Sheep Company
Eaton, Colorado

LAMB KEBOBS

♦ Prize-winning recipe at the Washakie County Lamb Cook-Off, Washakie County, Wyoming

Makes about 4 servings

MARINADE
  1 medium-size onion, chopped
  ³/₄ cup vegetable oil
  ¹/₂ cup dry red wine
  ¹/₄ cup lemon juice
  1 teaspoon salt
  2 cloves garlic, finely chopped
  1 bay leaf
  6 peppercorns

KEBOBS
  1 to 1¹/₂ pounds boneless lamb, cut into 1-inch cubes
    Mushrooms, whole if small, halved if large
    Green bell pepper, cut into strips
    Red bell pepper, cut into strips
    Cherry tomatoes
    Onion wedges, parboiled
    Celery chunks, parboiled
    Zucchini, sliced, or cut into chunks if small
    Pineapple chunks
    Apple chunks, unpeeled

  Melted butter (optional)
  Hot cooked rice, for serving

Parboiling vegetables means to boil them in water until they are almost halfway cooked. They are then drained and rinsed in cold water to stop further cooking. This process tenderizes long-cooking vegetables so their final cooking time will be less and they can then be combined with quicker cooking ingredients. Stir-fries and kebobs are two examples of dishes that can benefit from parboiling.

Combine all the marinade ingredients in a large glass jar with a tightly fitting lid; cover and shake well. Let stand at room temperature for 2 hours, shaking occasionally. Place the lamb in a baking dish and pour the marinade over it, making sure it is entirely covered by marinade. Cover and marinate in the refrigerator overnight.

Light a charcoal grill and begin cooking when the coals are medium-hot.* Remove the meat from the marinade; reserve the marinade. Thread cubes of lamb on skewers alternately with your choice of vegetables and fruits, taking care not to crowd the food. Grill the kebobs 4 inches from the coals until the meat is browned and the vegetables and fruits are tender, turning with long-handled tongs. Baste frequently with the reserved marinade or melted butter. Serve on a bed of hot rice.

Coals are medium-hot when you can **cautiously hold the palm of your hand 4 inches above the coals for a count of 3 seconds.*

Nancy Quinn
Ten Sleep, Wyoming

ZIPPY LAMB SHANKS

♦ Second place winner at the Natrona County Woolgrowers Lamb Cook-Off, Natrona County, Wyoming

Makes about 4 servings

 4 lamb shanks (2¹/₂ pounds each)
  Salt and pepper to taste
 2 tablespoons shortening
 1 medium-size onion, sliced
 ¹/₂ cup chopped celery
 ¹/₂ cup ketchup
 ¹/₂ cup water
 1¹/₂ teaspoons Worcestershire sauce
 ¹/₂ teaspoon garlic powder
  Hot cooked rice, for serving

Season the lamb with salt and pepper. Melt the shortening in a large heavy saucepan over medium heat. Add the shanks and cook until browned on all sides. Combine the onion, celery, ketchup, water, Worcestershire sauce and garlic powder in a small bowl; pour over the lamb. Reduce the heat; simmer, covered, for 1¹/₂ hours or until tender. Skim off the fat and serve with hot rice.

Joyce Snedden
Casper, Wyoming

LAMB RICE PILAF

♦ First place winner at the Natrona County Woolgrowers Lamb Cook-Off, Natrona County, Wyoming

Makes about 6 servings

 1 cup uncooked rice
 1 cup chicken or beef bouillon
 1 cup frozen peas
 1 cup thinly sliced fresh mushrooms
 2 tablespoons butter
 2 medium-size onions, finely chopped
 2 pounds lamb shoulder roast, cut into bite-sized cubes
  Salt and pepper to taste
  Garlic salt to taste
 1 cup sour cream
 ¹/₂ to 1 cup red wine
  Fresh seasonal vegetables, for garnish

Place the rice and bouillon in a medium-sized saucepan and bring to a boil; add the peas and mushrooms. Cover; reduce the heat and simmer gently for about 20 minutes or until all the liquid has been absorbed.

Melt the butter in a large skillet over medium heat. Add the onions and cook until softened. Add the lamb and season with salt, pepper and garlic salt; cook until the meat is browned. Add the rice mixture and simmer until the lamb is tender. Add the sour cream and cook gently until thickened; *do not boil.* Stir in ¹/₂ cup of the red wine. Taste and add additional wine as needed. Garnish with fresh seasonal vegetables.

Anita Wilson

Sour cream will curdle if it becomes too hot and there are no culinary tricks that will restore it. Always add sour cream at the end of the cooking time and heat it only until it is warm, not hot, and never to a boil.

SPECIAL LAMB MEATBALLS

♦ Prize-winning recipe at the High Country Lamb Cook-Off, Greeley, Colorado

Serves 6

    1 (15-ounce) can tomato sauce
 ¹/₂ cup packed brown sugar
 ¹/₄ cup finely chopped onion
    1 tablespoon Worcestershire sauce
    1 tablespoon vinegar
1¹/₂ pounds ground lamb
      Salt and pepper to taste
      Seasoned salt to taste
      Hot cooked rice or noodles, for serving

Combine the tomato sauce, sugar, onion, Worcestershire sauce and vinegar in a small saucepan; heat thoroughly. Set aside. Season the lamb with salt, pepper and seasoned salt; form into 1-inch balls. Place the meatballs in a heavy saucepan and cook over medium heat until well browned. Drain and discard the excess fat. Add the sauce mixture to the meatballs. Heat through and serve over hot rice or noodles, or serve as an appetizer.

Debbie Fitch

VEGETABLES & SIDE DISHES

BAKED PAPAYA UNCLE BEN'S®

Papaya is a tropical fruit native to the Americas. When ripe, the skin is usually deep yellow and the flesh is light orange to salmon colored with a soft texture. It can be served either raw or cooked. The center of the papaya contains lots of edible black seeds that have a peppery taste and can be used as a garnish or added to salad dressings. The flesh contains an enzyme called "papain" which is an ingredient in commercial meat tenderizers. If you make a gelatin mold with papaya, cook the fruit first or the papain will prevent it from gelling.

♦ Grand Prize winner in the Uncle Ben's® "Inn to Inn" Recipe Contest, sponsored by Uncle Ben's, Inc.

Makes 8 servings

2¹/₂ cups water
  1 cup Uncle Ben's® Converted Brand Rice
  1 teaspoon salt (optional)
  2 cups ricotta cheese
  1 tablespoon curry powder
  ¹/₂ cup very thinly sliced green onions
  ¹/₂ cup raisins
  ¹/₂ cup chopped mango chutney
  4 ripe papayas, halved lengthwise and seeded
  2 tablespoons sugar
  ¹/₂ teaspoon ground cinnamon
  ¹/₃ cup (²/₃ stick) butter, melted

Preheat the oven to 450°F. Bring the water to a boil in a medium-sized saucepan. Stir in the rice and salt. Reduce the heat; cover tightly and simmer for 20 minutes. Remove from the heat and let stand, covered, for about 5 minutes or until all the water is absorbed. Let the rice cool slightly.

Combine the ricotta cheese and curry powder in a large bowl; mix well. Stir in the rice, green onions, raisins and chutney. Spoon about ¹/₂ cup of the rice mixture into the hollow of each papaya half. Combine the sugar and cinnamon; sprinkle evenly over the tops, then drizzle with the melted butter. Place the filled papaya halves on a baking sheet. Bake for 15 minutes or until heated through.

The Cliff House
Mussel Shoals, California

RAINBOW ROOM'S LEMON PASTA

♦ Prize winner in "Casseroles of the Century" Pasta Contest, sponsored by the North Dakota Wheat Commission and North Dakota Mill, Bismarck, North Dakota

Makes 6 to 8 servings

    1 pound uncooked pasta of your choice
    11 tablespoons butter, divided
    12 stalks asparagus, cooked and cut into 1-inch pieces
    1 cup white wine
    2 to 3 shallots,* finely chopped
     Juice of 2 lemons
     Grated rind of 3 lemons, divided
    3 cups heavy cream
    3 tablespoons grated Parmesan cheese
     Salt and freshly ground pepper to taste
    1 tablespoon chopped parsley or chives

Cook the pasta in rapidly boiling salted water until tender, yet firm. Drain and keep warm. Melt 1 tablespoon of the butter in a large skillet over medium heat. Add the asparagus and sauté for a few minutes; drain on paper towels and set aside. Pour the wine into the same pan; add the shallots. Cook over high heat, stirring frequently, until the liquid is reduced by half. Add the lemon juice, grated rind of 2 lemons, the cream, 8 tablespoons of the butter cut into small pieces and the cheese. Reduce the heat and simmer, whisking constantly, for 3 to 4 minutes or until the sauce has thickened. Season with salt and pepper.

Place the sauce, pasta and remaining 2 tablespoons butter in a large bowl; toss to combine. Toss in the asparagus. Sprinkle the parsley and remaining lemon rind over the top and serve.

*Two tablespoons finely chopped onion may be substituted for the shallots.

National Pasta Association
Arlington, Virginia

Top to bottom: Rainbow Room's Lemon Pasta,
Fettuccine with Broccoli (page 120)

Pairing Side Dishes with Entrées

There are three equally important factors to consider when composing a plate: the texture, color and flavor of the side dishes should complement the entrée. For example, if the meat is crisp, choose a soft vegetable; if it is white, serve a colorful one. If you are serving chicken with a tomato sauce, take a moment to think how beets would look on the same plate and then choose a green vegetable instead. When a rich cream sauce is part of the entrée, the side dish should be less rich and have a contrasting flavor. A moment of thought in this direction is always worthwhile, for it can make the difference between a ho-hum meal and one that is really great.

FETTUCCINE WITH BROCCOLI

♦ Prize winner in "Casseroles of the Century" Pasta Contest, sponsored by the North Dakota Wheat Commission and North Dakota Mill, Bismarck, North Dakota

Makes 6 to 8 servings

1 large head broccoli (about 2 pounds), separated into flowerets
2 tablespoons olive oil
2 teaspoons butter
2 cloves garlic, very finely chopped
1/4 teaspoon red pepper flakes, or to taste
1 pound uncooked fettuccine
3/4 cup chopped walnuts
1/2 cup sliced pitted ripe olives
1/2 teaspoon salt
1/4 teaspoon freshly ground black pepper
1/4 cup freshly grated Parmesan cheese
1/4 cup freshly grated provolone cheese

Add the broccoli flowerets to boiling salted water and cook, covered, for 2 to 3 minutes or just until tender-crisp. Drain and keep warm. Heat the oil and butter in a small saucepan over very low heat; add the garlic and cook for about 2 minutes. Do not let the garlic brown. Add the red pepper flakes and set aside.

Preheat the oven to 350°F. Generously oil a large casserole or baking dish. Cook the pasta in rapidly boiling salted water until tender yet firm; drain. Toss the pasta with the garlic-butter sauce in a large heated bowl. Add the broccoli, walnuts, olives, salt and black pepper. Gradually add the Parmesan cheese, tossing to combine. Pour the pasta mixture into the prepared casserole; sprinkle the provolone cheese over the top. Bake for 5 to 10 minutes or until the cheese melts. Serve immediately.

Blanche Babinski
Minot, North Dakota

JOZE CURRIED SPROUTS

♦ Winner of Best Recipe Award at the Brussels Sprouts Harvest Festival, Santa Cruz, California

Makes 8 to 10 servings

- **2 to 3 pounds brussels sprouts, halved**
- **4 tablespoons (1/2 stick) butter**
- **1/4 cup peanut oil**
- **3 medium-size onions, finely chopped**
- **2 to 3 tablespoons turmeric***
- **2 to 3 tablespoons paprika***
- **2 teaspoons ground cinnamon**
- **1 to 2 tablespoons ground cumin***
- **2 teaspoons ground coriander**
- **1 teaspoon asafetida****
- **2 (14-ounce) cans coconut milk**
- **1 (28-ounce) can crushed tomatoes**

Steam or simmer the brussels sprouts 4 to 6 minutes or until just tender; drain and reserve. Heat the butter and oil in a large pot over medium heat. Add the onions and cook for 10 to 15 minutes or until soft and slightly golden; do not let them brown. Add the spices and asafetida; cook and stir for 2 to 3 minutes or until the aroma becomes slightly nutty. Do not let the spices burn. Add the coconut milk and tomatoes; bring to a simmer. Do not boil or the coconut milk may separate. Stir in the reserved sprouts and serve.

The quantities of these spices are approximate; the amount you use depends on your personal taste and the freshness and strength of the spices. This recipe should produce a spicy aroma but will not be particularly hot.

**Asafetida is a strong-tasting resinous gum and is available in some specialty shops. Four cloves of very finely chopped garlic may be substituted.*

Note: This dish makes an excellent main course if cooked chicken or tofu is added. It goes well with rice—especially Indian basmati rice, which is available in health food stores and specialty shops.

India Joze
Santa Cruz, California

Turmeric is a spice that is related to ginger. Because of its intense golden mustard color, it is also used as a dye. Turmeric is an essential component of curry powder and was once known as Indian saffron. Use it sparingly —a little turmeric goes a long way.

Before it became commonplace to transport fruits and vegetables from one region to another, winter vegetables were in short supply. Brussels sprouts, which are part of the hardy cabbage family, were often the only green vegetable available during the winter in Britain, Belgium, Holland and northern France. For the best flavor, look for tightly closed buds with fresh green leaves.

SWISS POTATO TORTE ▶

♦ Third place winner in the Side Dish category at the "Tabletalk" Cooking Contest, sponsored by *The Independence Examiner*, Independence, Missouri

Makes 6 servings

  3 tablespoons butter, softened
  6 medium-size potatoes, peeled and thinly sliced
1/2 cup grated Parmesan cheese
  1 teaspoon ground nutmeg
  1 teaspoon salt
1/4 teaspoon pepper
  2 cups (8 ounces) shredded Swiss cheese
1/4 cup heavy cream, warmed
    Chopped parsley and paprika, for garnish

Preheat the oven to 400°F. Generously grease a 2-quart ovenproof bowl with the butter. Alternately layer the potatoes, Parmesan cheese, nutmeg, salt, pepper and Swiss cheese in the prepared dish. Bake, tightly covered, for 1¼ hours or until the potatoes are tender. Let stand for 10 minutes, then invert onto a serving platter. Drizzle the warm cream over the top and garnish with parsley and paprika.

Nancy Barr
Independence, Missouri

Genuine Swiss cheese from Switzerland is known as Emmentaler. It is easy enough to produce the holes in the cheese, but difficult to produce the fine, nutty flavor that is its trademark. This characteristic flavor is said to be derived from the quality of the grasses on which the cattle feed. Both an eating and cooking cheese, it is often paired with grated Parmesan.

MICROWAVED CHEESE-ONION POTATOES

♦ Seventh prize winner in "The Secret's in the Soup" Recipe Contest, sponsored by Thomas J. Lipton, Inc.

Makes about 10 servings

  1 envelope Lipton® Onion Recipe Soup Mix
1/4 cup all-purpose flour
1/2 teaspoon salt
1/4 teaspoon pepper
  5 cups thinly sliced potatoes (about 2 pounds)
  3 tablespoons butter or margarine, cut into small
    pieces
1½ cups (6 ounces) shredded Cheddar cheese, divided
1½ cups water
  1 cup undiluted evaporated milk   *(continued)*

Potatoes rank first among the most important agricultural products in Western Europe and the Americas. On a worldwide level, they are second only to wheat. Potatoes are one of the 15 crops that feed the entire world.

MICROWAVE COOKING DIRECTIONS:
Combine the soup mix, flour, salt and pepper in a small bowl. Combine the potatoes, soup mixture, butter and 1 cup of the cheese in a 3-quart microwavable casserole; pour the water over the mixture. Microwave, uncovered, on High (100% power) for 25 minutes or until the potatoes are tender, stirring occasionally. Stir in the milk and microwave on High for 12 minutes or until the sauce is thickened, stirring occasionally. Top with the remaining ¹/2 cup cheese; microwave on High 1 minute or until the cheese is melted. Let stand, covered, for 5 minutes before serving.

Mary Bosworth
Pascagoula, Mississippi

TURNIP CASSEROLE

The turnip is a root vegetable that has never achieved the popularity of the potato, even though it can be mashed, baked, boiled, steamed and served in many of the same ways as potatoes. Select small, young turnips for a mild, sweet flavor and crisp texture. Older turnips can be woody and bitter.

♦ Finalist in the Vegetables category in the annual recipe contest sponsored by the *Reflector-Chronicle*, Abilene, Kansas

Makes 6 servings

4 cups peeled and sliced turnips
¹/4 cup chopped onion
2 teaspoons sugar
2 eggs, beaten
1 (10³/4-ounce) can condensed cream of mushroom soup
¹/2 cup cracker crumbs
1 tablespoon grated Parmesan cheese
4 tablespoons (¹/2 stick) margarine, melted

Preheat the oven to 350°F. Lightly grease a 2-quart casserole. Place the turnips, onion and sugar in a large saucepan; add water to cover and bring to a boil over high heat. Reduce the heat and simmer until the turnips are tender but not soft; drain. Combine the turnips, eggs and soup in a large bowl; mix well. Spoon into the prepared casserole. Sprinkle with the cracker crumbs and cheese. Drizzle the margarine over the top. Bake for 30 minutes or until the top is golden brown.

Jeanne Freeman
Abilene, Kansas

MICROWAVED PECAN CRISP SQUASH

♦ Finalist in the Microwave category at the "Tabletalk" Cooking Contest, sponsored by *The Independence Examiner*, Independence, Missouri

Makes 2 servings

   1 large acorn squash
   10 soda crackers, crushed into crumbs
   1/3 cup packed brown sugar
   1/4 cup chopped pecans
   4 tablespoons (1/2 stick) margarine
   1 teaspoon ground cinnamon
   1 teaspoon ground nutmeg

MICROWAVE COOKING DIRECTIONS:

Cut the acorn squash in half; remove and discard the seeds and fibers. Place the halves in a microwave oven and microwave on High (100% power) for 6 minutes.

Combine the remaining ingredients in a small microwavable bowl. Microwave on High for 30 seconds. Fill the squash cavities with the pecan mixture; microwave on High for 6 minutes or until the squash is tender. Cover with waxed paper and let stand 5 minutes before serving.

Jean Swann
Independence, Missouri

Acorn squash is an acorn-shaped winter squash with dark green fluted skin and yellow to orange flesh. Its large seed cavity makes it perfect for stuffing. Recently a miniature variety has become available. This smaller version is wonderful accompanied with applesauce and cinnamon—allow at least two squash per person.

Entire cookbooks have been devoted to zucchini because anyone who grows it is inevitably faced with an overabundance. Expert gardeners usually recommend eating this fast-growing vegetable when it is no more than five inches in length. It can be steamed, fried, stuffed or eaten raw.

ITALIAN ZUCCHINI CRESCENT PIE

♦ Grand Prize winner at the Pillsbury BAKE-OFF® Contest in Miami, Florida

Makes 6 servings

2 tablespoons margarine or butter
4 cups thinly sliced zucchini
1 cup chopped onion
2 tablespoons parsley flakes
1/2 teaspoon salt
1/2 teaspoon pepper
1/4 teaspoon garlic powder
1/4 teaspoon dried basil
1/4 teaspoon dried oregano
2 eggs, well beaten
2 cups (8 ounces) shredded Muenster or mozzarella cheese
1 (8-ounce) can Pillsbury Refrigerated Quick Crescent Dinner Rolls
2 teaspoons prepared mustard

Preheat the oven to 375°F. Melt the margarine in a 10-inch skillet over medium heat. Add the zucchini and onion; cook for about 8 minutes or until tender. Stir in the parsley flakes, salt, pepper, garlic powder, basil and oregano. Combine the eggs and cheese in a large bowl; mix well. Stir in the cooked vegetable mixture.

Separate the crescent dough into 8 triangles.* Place in an ungreased 10-inch pie plate, 12 × 8-inch baking dish or 11-inch quiche dish; press over the bottom and up the sides to form a crust. Firmly press the perforations together to seal. Spread the mustard over the crust and evenly pour in the egg mixture. Bake for 18 to 22 minutes or until a knife inserted near the center comes out clean. If necessary, cover the crust with foil during the last 10 minutes of baking to prevent excessive browning. Let the pie stand for 10 minutes before serving.

*If a 12 × 8-inch baking dish is used, unroll and separate the dough into 2 long rectangles; press over the bottom and 1 inch up the sides to form the crust. Firmly press the perforations together to seal. Continue as directed above.

Millicent Caplan
Tamarac, Florida

Peeling Tomatoes

To peel tomatoes, place them, one at a time, in a saucepan of simmering water for about 10 seconds. (Add about 30 seconds if they are not fully ripened.) Then immediately plunge them into a bowl of cold water for another 10 seconds. The skins will peel off easily with a knife. Do not add more than one tomato at a time to the water or the temperature will drop rapidly and the tomatoes will stew before their skins can be removed.

SCRAMBLED CABBAGE ▸

♦ Finalist in the Vegetables category in the annual recipe contest sponsored by the *Reflector-Chronicle*, Abilene, Kansas

Makes 8 servings

  3 tablespoons vegetable oil or bacon drippings
  1 clove garlic, very finely chopped
  3 cups finely shredded green cabbage (¹/₂ medium-size head)
  2 medium-size tomatoes, peeled and cut into cubes
  1 medium-size onion, thinly sliced
  1 cup thinly sliced celery
  1 cup frozen corn
¹/₂ cup chopped green bell pepper
  1 teaspoon sugar
  1 teaspoon salt
  1 teaspoon dill weed (optional)
¹/₄ teaspoon black pepper

Heat the oil in a large skillet over medium heat. Add the garlic and cook for 1 minute. Stir in the cabbage, tomatoes, onion, celery, corn and green pepper. Sprinkle with the seasonings. Cover and cook for 5 to 8 minutes or until the vegetables are crisp-tender, stirring once or twice during cooking.

Lavonne Geist
Abilene, Kansas

Along with corn,

lima beans are a primary ingredient of the Indian dish succotash. Different varieties of lima beans are known in the South as butter beans and calico beans. Lima beans are usually sold frozen or canned and are rarely seen fresh on the market.

EXTRA-DELICIOUS BEANS ▸

♦ Finalist in the Vegetables category in the annual recipe contest sponsored by the *Reflector-Chronicle*, Abilene, Kansas

Serves 14

  3 (10-ounce) packages frozen lima beans
  6 slices bacon, diced
  1 cup packed brown sugar
³/₄ cup ketchup
  1 (16-ounce) can butter beans, drained
     Heavy cream

(continued)

Preheat the oven to 350°F. Cook the lima beans in salted water until tender; drain thoroughly. Fry the bacon in a small skillet until crisp; drain on paper towels. Combine the sugar and ketchup in a small bowl. Combine the lima and butter beans and the bacon in a large bowl; stir in the sugar mixture. Spoon into a large shallow casserole; pour over just enough heavy cream to come up to the edge of the beans. Bake for about 1 hour.

Joan Donahue
Lincolnville, Kansas

MUSHROOMS FLORENTINE ▸

Recently there has been an explosion of mushrooms in the marketplace. In fancy produce stores you can now find many varieties of mushrooms both fresh and dried—cepes, chanterelles, enoki, morels, shiitake and porcini, to name just a few. The domestic white button mushroom, however, continues to be the most popular and widely available. Choose button mushrooms that have caps tightly closed around the stems; the dark interior of the caps should not be showing.

♦ Second place winner at the Mushroom Cook-Off, sponsored by the Pennsylvania Fresh Mushroom Program, Kennett Square, Pennsylvania

Serves 6 to 8

   4 tablespoons (1/2 stick) butter, melted, divided
   1 pound medium-size whole mushrooms
   1 teaspoon salt
   1/4 cup finely chopped onion
   2 (10-ounce) packages frozen chopped spinach, thawed
      and drained
   1 cup (4 ounces) shredded Cheddar cheese, divided
      Garlic salt to taste

Preheat the oven to 350°F. Place 2 tablespoons of the butter in a large skillet over medium heat. Add the mushrooms and cook until browned, browning the cap sides first. Stir the salt, onion and remaining 2 tablespoons butter into the spinach. Line a 10-inch casserole with the spinach mixture. Sprinkle 1/2 cup of the cheese over the spinach. Arrange the browned mushrooms over the cheese; season with the garlic salt and top with the remaining 1/2 cup cheese. Bake for 20 minutes or until the cheese is melted and browned. Serve hot.

Mrs. Robert Waterhose
Wilmington, Delaware

FRESH CORN PUDDING

◆ Prize-winning recipe at the March of Dimes Gourmet Gala in New York, New York

Makes about 10 servings

2 tablespoons butter, melted
10 ears fresh corn, husks and silk removed
6 eggs
2 cups half-and-half
1/2 cup all-purpose flour
2 tablespoons sugar
   Salt and white pepper to taste
1 teaspoon ground nutmeg
4 tablespoons (1/2 stick) butter, softened
   Pimientos, cut into triangles, for garnish
   Parsley sprigs, for garnish

Corn is a native American food. When the English arrived in America, they called this yellow grain of the Indians "corn" because it was their generic term for grain or things that were small. The settlers soon learned to make a variety of tasty corn dishes, including bread and pudding. To the Pilgrims, fresh corn pudding served with maple syrup was the equivalent of today's premium ice cream—and eaten as frequently.

Grease a round 10 × 2-inch baking dish with the melted butter; set aside. With a sharp knife, scrape upward on each ear of corn over a medium-sized bowl to slice off the kernels. Then, with the back of the knife, scrape downward to remove the remaining part of the kernels and the liquid from the cob. (You should have 3 1/2 to 4 cups of kernels.)

Preheat the oven to 375°F. Place the corn kernels, eggs, half-and-half, flour, sugar, salt and pepper in the work bowl of a food processor. Process for 4 or 5 seconds, using a few on/off turns, until pureed. Pour the egg mixture into the prepared baking dish. Sprinkle the nutmeg over the top and dot with the softened butter. Place the baking dish in a larger pan and pour in enough hot water to come halfway up the sides of the baking dish. Bake for 1 hour or until a knife inserted into the center comes out clean. Garnish with pimientos and parsley sprigs.

Aileen Mehle

BREADS

CRANBERRY-WALNUT MUFFINS

♦ Third prize winner in the Muffins category in the Make It Better with Cranberries Contest, sponsored by the Cape Cod Cranberry Growers' Association, the Massachusetts Department of Food & Agriculture and Cranberry World Visitors Center, Plymouth, Massachusetts

Makes about 1¹/₂ dozen muffins

 8 tablespoons (1 stick) butter, softened
1¹/₂ cups sugar
 2 eggs
2¹/₄ cups all-purpose flour
 2 teaspoons baking powder
 ¹/₂ teaspoon salt
 ¹/₂ cup milk
2¹/₂ cups chopped fresh cranberries
 ¹/₂ cup chopped walnuts

Preheat the oven to 350°F. Grease 2¹/₂-inch muffin cups. Cream the butter and sugar in a medium-sized bowl until fluffy. Blend in the eggs, one at a time. Combine the flour, baking powder and salt in a small bowl; stir into the butter mixture. Gradually add the milk; mix thoroughly. Stir in the cranberries and walnuts. Spoon the batter evenly into the prepared muffin cups. Bake for 25 to 30 minutes or until golden brown. Remove the muffins to wire racks to cool.

Gerry Griffith
South Carver, Massachusetts

Top to bottom: Maple Oatmeal Bread (page 153), Cranberry-Walnut Muffins, Braided Cinnamon Loaf (page 146)

The National Date Festival, held in the tiny town of Indio in Southern California, is the only fair in the country that features camel and ostrich races. Nearly 200,000 visitors flock to the festivities and watch the snake charmer and the Arabian Nights Pageant.

OATMEAL-DATE MUFFINS

♦ Finalist in the Quick Breads category at the National Date Festival, Indio, California

Makes 1 dozen muffins

1¼ cups all-purpose flour
⅓ cup sugar
1 tablespoon baking powder
1 teaspoon salt
1 cup uncooked rolled oats
½ cup chopped pitted dates
1 egg
1 cup milk
⅓ cup melted shortening or butter

Preheat the oven to 400°F. Grease 12 (2½-inch) muffin cups. Mix the flour, sugar, baking powder and salt in a large bowl. Stir in the oats and dates. Beat the egg in a small bowl; stir in the milk and shortening. Add the milk mixture to the flour mixture and stir just until the dry ingredients are moistened. Do not overmix; the batter will be lumpy. Spoon the batter evenly into the prepared muffin cups. Bake for 20 to 25 minutes or until browned. Remove the muffins from the pans and serve hot.

Rosie L. Dean
Thermal, California

Crisp, tart, juicy Granny Smith apples are not only delicious eaten raw, but are also excellent for baking because they keep their texture. And unlike other apples, you can enjoy these green-skinned beauties year-round. After the fall American-grown crop is consumed, the harvest from New Zealand and Australia arrives in spring.

APPLE BREAD

♦ Prize winner in the fifth- to sixth-grade category in the Apple Recipe Contest for Grades 5 through 12, sponsored by *The Hartford Courant*, Hartford, Connecticut

Makes 1 loaf

2 cups all-purpose flour
1 cup sugar, divided
1 tablespoon baking powder
½ teaspoon salt
1 cup milk
1 egg
4 tablespoons (½ stick) butter, melted
2 Granny Smith apples, peeled, cored and diced
½ cup chopped walnuts
2 teaspoons ground cinnamon, divided
1 slice bread, made into crumbs

Preheat the oven to 350°F. Butter a 9×5×3-inch loaf pan. Combine the flour, 1/2 cup of the sugar, the baking powder and salt in a large bowl. Combine the milk, egg and butter in a small bowl. Add to the flour mixture and stir just until moistened; do not overmix. Toss the apples with 1/4 cup of the sugar, the walnuts and 1 teaspoon of the cinnamon; stir into the batter. Pour into the prepared pan. Combine the remaining 1/4 cup sugar, 1 teaspoon cinnamon and the bread crumbs in a small bowl; sprinkle over the top of the batter. Bake for 1 hour or until a toothpick inserted into the center comes out clean. Cool the bread in the pan on a wire rack for 10 minutes. Loosen the edges and remove from the pan; cool completely on a wire rack.

Lisa Zahren
Simsbury, Connecticut

CRANBERRY-BANANA BREAD

♦ First prize winner in the Breads category in the Make It Better with Cranberries Contest, sponsored by the Cape Cod Cranberry Growers' Association, the Massachusetts Department of Food & Agriculture and Cranberry World Visitors Center, Plymouth, Massachusetts

Makes 1 loaf

1³/₄ **cups all-purpose flour**
  1 **tablespoon baking powder**
 ³/₄ **cup sugar**
 ¹/₂ **cup shortening**
  2 **eggs**
  1 **cup mashed ripe bananas**
1¹/₄ **cups coarsely chopped fresh cranberries**

Preheat the oven to 350°F. Grease and flour a 9×5×3-inch loaf pan. Mix the flour and baking powder in a small bowl; set aside. Beat the sugar, shortening and eggs in a medium-sized bowl until light and fluffy. Mix in the bananas and cranberries. Add the dry ingredients, stirring just until smooth; do not overmix. Pour into the prepared pan. Bake for 50 to 60 minutes or until golden brown and a toothpick inserted into the center comes out clean. Cool the bread in the pan on a wire rack for 15 minutes. Loosen the edges and remove from the pan; cool completely on a wire rack.

Linda Shea
Whitman, Massachusetts

Cranberries are native to North America. Pilgrims noticed that the cranes flew to the cranberry bogs in great flocks and feasted on the sour red berries. Thus they got their name—not craneberries but cranberries.

Making Vanilla Sugar

To make vanilla sugar, place one or two vanilla beans in a small canister of granulated sugar. Keep the canister tightly closed for a few weeks or until the sugar is infused with the flavor of vanilla. You can continue to replenish the sugar in the canister until the beans lose their flavoring power. Substitute vanilla sugar for plain sugar whenever a sweet vanilla flavor is desired.

FRUITED RICOTTA BREAD

♦ First prize winner in the Quick Breads category in the Holiday Breads Contest, sponsored by *The Hartford Courant*, Hartford, Connecticut

Makes 1 loaf

4 cups all-purpose flour
2 teaspoons baking powder
2 cups ricotta cheese
3 eggs
2/3 cup granulated sugar
3 tablespoons chopped mixed candied fruit
2 tablespoons golden raisins
2 tablespoons vanilla sugar, divided
1 tablespoon grated lemon rind
1 tablespoon chopped almonds
  Pinch of salt
1 tablespoon butter, melted
1 tablespoon powdered sugar

Preheat the oven to 350°F. Grease and flour a baking sheet. Sift the flour with the baking powder into a large bowl; form a well in the center. Add the ricotta, eggs, granulated sugar, candied fruit, raisins, 1 tablespoon of the vanilla sugar, the lemon rind, almonds and salt to the well. Mix to form a firm dough. Turn out onto a lightly floured surface and knead lightly. Shape into a loaf and place on the prepared baking sheet. Use a sharp knife to cut 3 slashes in the top of the loaf. Bake for 50 to 60 minutes or until a wooden skewer inserted into the center comes out clean. Transfer the bread to a wire rack. Brush the butter over the warm loaf. Mix the powdered sugar and remaining 1 tablespoon vanilla sugar; sift over the top of the buttered loaf.

Judith Forbes
East Hampton, Connecticut

*Left to right: Oatmeal-Date Muffins (page 136),
Fruited Ricotta Bread*

oney is one of the only foods that will never go bad, no matter how long you keep it. Be sure to store it in a tightly closed jar in a cool, dry place. Some amazing facts about honey according to the National Honey Board: How far does a hive of bees fly to bring us one pound of honey? Over 55,000 miles. And how much honey does the average worker honey bee make in its lifetime? One twelfth of a teaspoon.

HONEY BREAD

♦ Prize winner at the A-OK Cook-Off, sponsored by various Oklahoma agricultural associations, Oklahoma City, Oklahoma

Makes 2 small loaves

    1/2 cup water
    1/4 cup honey
      2 tablespoons shortening
      2 tablespoons packed brown sugar
      1 cup whole wheat flour
    1/2 cup all-purpose flour
    3/4 teaspoon baking soda
    1/4 teaspoon salt

Preheat the oven to 375°F. Combine the water, honey, shortening and sugar in a large bowl. Combine the flours, baking soda and salt in a small bowl. Gradually add the dry ingredients to the honey mixture; mix well. Divide the dough in half. Shape into 2 loaves on a lightly floured surface; place on an ungreased baking sheet. Bake for 10 to 12 minutes or until golden brown. Remove the loaves to a wire rack. Serve warm or cooled with butter.

Christie Patric
Francis Tuttle FHA/HERO, Oklahoma

DATE BREAD

♦ Second place winner in the Quick Breads category at the National Date Festival, Indio, California

Makes 1 loaf

      2 eggs
    1/4 cup packed light brown sugar
    1/4 cup granulated sugar
      1 tablespoon finely shredded orange rind
      4 cups self-rising flour
      1 pound fresh dates, pitted and chopped
      1 cup buttermilk

Preheat the oven to 325°F. Grease a 10-inch Bundt® or tube pan. Beat the eggs with the sugars and orange rind in a large bowl. Stir in the flour, dates and buttermilk; mix thoroughly. Pour the batter into the prepared pan;

place the pan on a large baking sheet. Bake for 1¹/₂ hours or until a toothpick inserted near the center comes out clean. Cool the bread in the pan on a wire rack for 10 minutes. Loosen the edge and turn it out onto a wooden board or platter to cool completely.

Mae M. Gruel
Escondido, California

ORANGE DATE CRESCENT CLAWS

♦ Prize winner at the Pillsbury BAKE-OFF® Contest in San Diego, California

Makes 8 rolls

¹/₂ cup chopped walnuts or pecans
¹/₄ cup sugar
 1 teaspoon grated orange rind
¹/₂ cup chopped pitted dates
 1 (8-ounce) can Pillsbury Refrigerated Quick Crescent
    Dinner Rolls
 2 tablespoons margarine or butter, melted, divided

Preheat the oven to 375°F. Combine the walnuts, sugar and orange rind in a small bowl and blend well. Reserve ¹/₄ cup of the mixture for a topping. Stir the dates into the remaining mixture and set aside.

Separate the crescent dough into 4 rectangles and firmly press the perforations to seal. Cut each rectangle in half crosswise; press or roll out each one to form eight 4-inch squares. Brush each with some of the margarine. Spoon about 2 tablespoonfuls of the date mixture across the center third of each square to within ¹/₄ inch of the edges. Fold the sides of the dough over the filling and pinch the center seam and ends to seal.

Place the rolls seam side down on an ungreased baking sheet. Using a scissors or sharp knife, make three ¹/₂-inch cuts in one folded edge of each roll. To form claws, separate the cut sections of each roll by gently curving into a crescent shape. Brush the top of each claw with the remaining margarine and sprinkle with the reserved sugar-nut mixture. Bake for 8 to 12 minutes or until golden brown.

Barbara Rhea
Beavercreek, Ohio

MUSHROOM CRESCENT ROLLS

♦ Third place winner at the Mushroom Cook-Off, sponsored by the Pennsylvania Fresh Mushroom Program, Kennett Square, Pennsylvania

Makes 16 rolls

   3 tablespoons butter
   1 medium-size onion, finely chopped
   1/2 pound mushrooms, finely chopped
   1/4 cup sour cream
   2 tablespoons all-purpose flour
   1/2 teaspoon salt
   1/2 teaspoon pepper
   1/4 teaspoon dried thyme
   2 (8-ounce) cans refrigerated crescent dinner rolls

Preheat the oven to 350°F. Melt the butter in a medium-sized saucepan. Add the onion and cook over medium heat until softened. Add the mushrooms and cook for 3 minutes. Remove from the heat and stir in the sour cream, flour, salt, pepper and thyme. Separate the crescent rolls into 16 triangles. Spread the mushroom mixture evenly over the triangles, then roll up according to the package directions. Bake for 15 to 20 minutes or until golden brown.

Linda Wedlock
Oxford, Pennsylvania

Americans are wild about doughnuts! If you've never made them at home, you'll be surprised at how much better they taste than store-bought doughnuts. When frying them, be sure to keep the oil at a constant temperature. If you add too many doughnuts to the oil at once, the temperature will drop causing the doughnuts to absorb the oil and become greasy. And don't forget to fry the doughnut holes!

Every April in Vermont, when the snow is often still thick on the ground, a great maple festival takes place. There are maple-glazed doughnuts, maple-sugar candy, pancakes drenched in maple syrup and as much maple fudge to eat as a body can bear. And, of course, there's a cooking contest where the winner is crowned Mrs. Maple, the Maple Queen.

MAPLE DELIGHT

♦ Winner of the Mrs. Maple award at the Vermont Maple Festival, St. Albans, Vermont

Makes about 4 dozen doughnuts

1/2 cup maple syrup
1/2 cup milk
1 teaspoon salt
1/4 cup sugar
4 tablespoons (1/2 stick) butter
1 package active dry yeast
1/4 cup warm water (105° to 115°F)
3/4 cup unseasoned mashed potatoes
2 eggs, beaten
5 cups all-purpose flour, divided
    Vegetable oil, for deep-frying
    Maple syrup, for glazing

Heat the 1/2 cup maple syrup, the milk and salt in a small saucepan over low heat until bubbles form around the edge of the pan. Remove from the heat and add the sugar and butter, stirring until the butter is melted; cool to 105° to 115°F. Dissolve the yeast in the water in a large bowl. Add the warm milk mixture, the potatoes, eggs and 2 cups of the flour. Beat for 2 minutes or until smooth. Add the remaining 3 cups flour and combine thoroughly. Cover with a towel and let rise in a warm place (85°F) until doubled, for about 1 hour.

Punch down the dough. Turn out onto a lightly floured surface and knead slightly. Roll out dough 1/4 inch thick and cut out with a doughnut cutter. Using a spatula, transfer the doughnuts to a floured towel. Cover and let rise until doubled, for about 30 minutes.

Heat the oil in a deep-fat fryer to 375°F. Fry the doughnuts, a few at a time, for about 2 minutes or until golden brown on both sides. Drain on paper towels.

Make a glaze by cooking some maple syrup in a large pan until it reaches 235°F on a candy thermometer. Do not stir the syrup while it is cooking. Remove from the heat; pour onto a baking sheet and cool to 60°F, then stir until very creamy. Spread the glaze on the doughnuts while warm.

Nancy Cadieux

Braided Cinnamon Loaf

♦ First place in the Bread category of the Culinary Department at the Kentucky State Fair, Louisville, Kentucky

Makes 2 loaves

DOUGH
  1 cup milk
  8 tablespoons (1 stick) butter or margarine
  1/2 cup granulated sugar
  1 tablespoon salt
  5 to 5 1/2 cups all-purpose flour, divided
  2 packages active dry yeast
  1/2 cup warm water (105° to 115°F)
  2 eggs, beaten

FILLING
  1/2 cup packed brown sugar
  1 1/2 teaspoons ground cinnamon
  2 tablespoons butter or margarine, softened

GLAZE
  1 generous cup powdered sugar
  2 tablespoons milk
  1 teaspoon almond extract

To make the dough, scald the 1 cup milk in a small saucepan over medium heat. Combine the milk, the 8 tablespoons butter, the granulated sugar and salt in a large bowl and cool until warm (105° to 115°F). Stir in 2 cups of the flour and beat until smooth. Dissolve the yeast in the water in a small bowl. Add the yeast mixture and eggs to the milk mixture, beating thoroughly. Add enough of the remaining flour to make the dough easy to handle. Turn out onto a lightly floured surface. Knead for 10 minutes or until the dough is smooth and elastic, adding as much remaining flour as needed to prevent sticking. Shape the dough into a ball. Place in a large greased bowl; turn the dough once to grease the surface. Cover with a towel and let rise in a warm place (85°F) until doubled, for about 1 hour.

Punch down the dough; divide in half and let rest 10 minutes. Meanwhile, make the filling by combining the brown sugar and cinnamon in a small bowl; add the 2 tablespoons butter and mix until creamy.

Roll half of the dough into an 18 × 8-inch rectangle. Make a series of cuts along the 18-inch sides of the dough at 2-inch intervals. Spread half of the filling down the center and fold the strips over the filling, alternating one strip from each side and overlapping the ends over the filling. Repeat with the remaining dough and filling. Place the loaves on greased baking sheets. Cover and let rise in a warm place until doubled, for about 30 minutes.

Preheat the oven to 350°F. Bake for 45 minutes or until golden brown. Remove from the baking sheets to wire racks. To make the glaze, combine the powdered sugar, the 2 tablespoons milk and the almond extract in a small bowl; brush over the loaves while still warm.

Geneva Hawkins
Louisville, Kentucky

COFFEE CAKE SQUARES

♦ First place winner in the Breads and Rolls category at the "Tabletalk" Cooking Contest, sponsored by *The Independence Examiner*, Independence, Missouri

Makes 8 servings

   1 package active dry yeast
  2/3 cup granulated sugar
   1 cup warm water (105° to 115°F)
   1 egg
   4 tablespoons (1/2 stick) butter or margarine, melted
   1 teaspoon grated orange rind
  1/2 teaspoon salt
  21/2 cups all-purpose flour, divided
  1/2 cup strawberry preserves, chilled
   1 cup powdered sugar
   2 tablespoons milk or orange juice
  2/3 cup pecan halves

Dissolve the yeast and granulated sugar in the water in a large bowl. Let stand for 5 minutes or until bubbly. Stir in the egg, butter, orange rind, salt and 11/2 cups of the flour until smooth. Stir in the remaining 1 cup flour until a stiff dough forms. Spread in a well-greased 10 × 8-inch pan. Let rise, uncovered, in a warm place (85°F) until doubled, for about 1 hour.

Preheat the oven to 375°F. Drop the strawberry preserves by teaspoonfuls over the dough; push the preserves lightly into the dough. Bake for 25 minutes or until golden brown. Cool in the pan on a wire rack.

Mix the powdered sugar and milk in a small bowl until smooth. Drizzle half of the mixture over the coffee cake. Top with the nuts, then drizzle the remaining glaze over the nuts. To serve, cut into squares.

Wynema Gwinn
Independence, Missouri

Freezing Bread

Let a freshly baked loaf cool for at least three hours on a wire rack before freezing. Place the loaf in the freezer on a flat surface for two hours or until it is solidly frozen. Wrap the frozen loaf in plastic wrap and then in heavy-duty aluminum foil. Label it with the date and the type of bread and return it to the freezer. Bread can be frozen for up to six months. Thaw frozen bread in its wrapping at room temperature for two to three hours. Freshen the loaf by heating it in a 300°F oven for 20 minutes.

SESAME-CHEESE BREAD

♦ Grand Prize winner at the "Tabletalk" Cooking Contest, sponsored by *The Independence Examiner*, Independence, Missouri

Makes 1 large loaf

   1 cup (4 ounces) shredded Cheddar cheese
   8 tablespoons (1 stick) butter, divided
   1/2 teaspoon garlic powder
   1/2 teaspoon Italian seasoning
   2 tablespoons sesame seeds
   1/2 cup milk
   1/2 cup water
2 1/2 cups all-purpose flour, divided
   2 packages active dry yeast
   2 tablespoons sugar
   1/2 teaspoon salt
   1 egg

Mix the cheese, 4 tablespoons of the butter, the garlic powder and Italian seasoning in a small bowl; set aside. Butter an 8-cup tube or Bundt® pan and sprinkle with the sesame seeds.

Heat the milk, water and the remaining 4 tablespoons butter in a small saucepan over low heat until very warm (120° to 130°F). Combine 1 1/2 cups of the flour, the yeast, sugar and salt in a large bowl; add the warm milk mixture. Add the egg and beat for 3 minutes at medium speed. Stir in the remaining 1 cup flour by hand to make a stiff, sticky dough. Spoon half of the dough into the prepared pan, spreading it fairly evenly. Crumble the cheese filling over the top, then cover with the remaining dough. Cover with waxed paper and let rise in a warm place (85°F) until doubled, for about 1 hour.

Preheat the oven to 350°F. Bake for 35 to 40 minutes or until golden brown. Immediately remove it from the pan to a wire rack to cool.

Debbie Oldenburg
Independence, Missouri

Kneading Bread Dough

The purpose of kneading yeast bread dough is to make it smooth and to develop the gluten. Gluten is a protein substance found in wheat flour that becomes elastic when kneaded; it gives the bread structure.

Knead bread dough on a lightly floured surface. Always use the heel of your hand to knead, not your fingers. Push the dough away from you with the heel of your hand, then bring the far end down to fold the dough in half. Give the dough a quarter turn and repeat the process, adding more flour as needed to prevent sticking. You should develop a rhythm to your kneading, making the motion fluid and continuous. Knead the dough until it is smooth, satiny and springs back when pressed with a finger, eight to ten minutes.

SAUSAGE-ONION BRAID

♦ First prize winner in the Yeast Breads category in the Holiday Breads Contest, sponsored by *The Hartford Courant*, Hartford, Connecticut

Makes 2 loaves

    5 tablespoons instant minced onion
    5 tablespoons water
    2 packages active dry yeast
 $1/4$ cup warm water (105° to 115°F)
    7 to $71/2$ cups all-purpose flour, divided
    2 pounds hot Italian sausage, cooked, crumbled and drained
    2 cups warm milk (105° to 115°F)
 $1/4$ cup sugar
    2 tablespoons butter or margarine
    1 tablespoon salt
 $21/2$ teaspoons garlic powder
    2 teaspoons dried oregano
 $1/2$ teaspoon pepper
    1 egg mixed with 1 tablespoon water

Combine the onion and 5 tablespoons water in a small bowl; let soak until all the water is absorbed. Dissolve the yeast in the warm water in a large bowl. Add the onions, 4 cups of the flour and all the remaining ingredients *except* the egg mixture; mix just until blended. Stir in enough of the remaining flour to make the dough easy to handle. Turn out onto a lightly floured surface. Knead for 10 minutes or until the dough is smooth and elastic, adding as much remaining flour as needed to prevent sticking. Shape the dough into a ball. Place in a large oiled bowl; turn the dough once to grease the surface. Cover with a towel and let rise in a warm place (85°F) until doubled, about 1 hour. Punch down the dough; turn out onto a lightly floured surface and knead slightly. Divide into 6 equal pieces. Shape each piece into a 15-inch rope. Make 2 braids, using 3 ropes for each braid. Pinch the ends under and place each braid on a greased baking sheet. Brush the loaves with some of the egg mixture; cover and let rise in a warm place until almost doubled. Preheat the oven to 375°F. Brush the loaves with the remaining egg mixture. Bake for 30 to 35 minutes or until they sound hollow when tapped. Remove from the sheets and cool on wire racks.

Pamela Backstrom
Windsor, Connecticut

Left to right:
Heartland Freezer Rye Bread (page 152),
Sausage-Onion Braid

The distinctive flavor of rye bread comes not from the rye flour, but from the caraway seeds that are almost always among the list of ingredients. Because rye flour contains practically no gluten—a protein substance in flour that helps bread achieve a light texture—it is usually combined with wheat flour in recipes. An exception is an authentic loaf of German pumpernickel bread; it is dark, dense and made entirely with rye flour.

HEARTLAND FREEZER RYE BREAD

♦ Grand Champion winner in the Illinois Blue Ribbon Culinary Contest at the Illinois State Fair, Springfield, Illinois

Makes 2 loaves

4 to 4¹/₂ cups bread flour, divided
2 cups rye flour
1 tablespoon salt
1 tablespoon caraway seeds, crushed
2 packages active dry yeast
4 tablespoons (¹/₂ stick) butter or margarine, softened
  or ¹/₄ cup vegetable oil
2 cups very warm water (120° to 130°F)
¹/₃ cup molasses
  Cornmeal
1 egg white plus 1 tablespoon water *or* softened butter
  or margarine, for glazing (optional)

Thoroughly mix 2 cups of the bread flour, the rye flour, salt, caraway seeds and yeast in a large bowl. Add the butter. Gradually add the water and molasses to the dry ingredients and beat for 3 minutes at medium speed, scraping the bowl occasionally. Stir in enough of the remaining bread flour to make a stiff dough. Turn out onto a lightly floured surface. Knead for 10 minutes or until the dough is smooth and elastic, adding as much remaining flour as needed to prevent sticking. At this point, the dough can either be frozen or raised and baked immediately. **To freeze the dough,** divide it in half. Form each half into a small round ball; flatten each ball into a 7-inch mound. Place on greased baking sheets; cover with plastic wrap and freeze until firm. Transfer to plastic bags and freeze up to 4 weeks. Remove the dough from the freezer and place on ungreased baking sheets that have been sprinkled with cornmeal. Cover and let stand at room temperature for about 2 hours and 15 minutes or until fully thawed. Let rise in a warm place (85°F) until doubled, for about 2 hours. Preheat the oven to 375°F. If using the egg white glaze, brush over the loaves and sprinkle with additional caraway seeds; slash the tops with a sharp knife. Bake for 15 minutes. *Reduce the heat to 350°F.* Bake for 20 minutes longer or until the loaves sound hollow when tapped. If using the butter to glaze, brush over the loaves. Remove from the sheets and cool on racks. **To use the dough immediately,** shape it into mounds as directed. Place on ungreased baking sheets that have been sprinkled with cornmeal; let rise in a warm place until almost doubled, for about 1 hour. If desired, glaze with the egg mixture as directed. Bake as directed. If using the butter glaze, brush over the loaves. Remove from the sheets and cool on racks.

Joan Sutor
Monmouth, Illinois

MAPLE OATMEAL BREAD

♦ Winner of the Mrs. Maple award at the Vermont Maple Festival, St. Albans, Vermont

Makes 2 loaves

    3 cups boiling water
    1 cup hot black coffee
    1 cup uncooked rolled oats
    1/2 cup maple syrup
    1/3 cup shortening
    1/4 cup sugar
    2 teaspoons salt
    2 packages active dry yeast
    1/4 cup warm water (105° to 115°F)
    2 eggs
5 1/2 to 6 cups all-purpose flour, divided

Combine the boiling water, coffee, oats, maple syrup, shortening, sugar and salt in a large bowl; cool to 105° to 115°F. Dissolve the yeast in the warm water in a small bowl; stir into the maple mixture. Blend in the eggs. Gradually add 2 1/2 cups of the flour and mix until smooth. Stir in enough of the remaining flour to make a stiff dough. Turn out onto a lightly floured surface. Knead for 10 minutes or until the dough is smooth and elastic, adding as much remaining flour as needed to prevent sticking. Shape the dough into a ball. Place in a large greased bowl; turn the dough once to grease the surface. Cover with a towel and let rise in a warm place (85°F) until doubled, for about 1 hour. Punch down the dough. Turn out onto a lightly floured surface and knead slightly; divide in half. Roll out each half into a 12 × 8-inch rectangle. Roll up the dough, beginning on an 8-inch side. Pinch the seams to seal and fold the ends under. Place in 2 greased 9 × 5 × 3-inch loaf pans. Cover; let rise in a warm place until doubled, for about 1 hour. Preheat the oven to 350°F. Bake for 45 minutes or until the loaves are browned and sound hollow when tapped. Remove from the pans and cool on racks.

Mary Boissoneault

Oatmeal is made by removing the hulls from whole oats. The resulting oat groats are then steamed and rolled to flatten them into flakes. Thus, they are often called rolled oats. Old-fashioned rolled oats and quick cooking rolled oats are essentially the same; the quick cooking oats simply cook faster because they have been rolled into thinner flakes. You can use quick cooking and old-fashioned oats interchangeably in most recipes.

COOKIES & CANDIES

Raisins are most often made from Thompson seedless grapes. Some have been dried naturally by the sun, although the majority are usually dried by artificial heat. They are loaded with sugar and crammed with vitamins and iron. When incorporating raisins into a batter or dough, dust them lightly with flour first. This will prevent them from sticking together and also from sinking to the bottom of the pan. Store leftover raisins in a tightly covered glass jar or place the opened package in an airtight plastic bag.

RAISIN-SPICE COOKIES

♦ First place winner in the Topsfield Fair Baking Competition, sponsored by the Essex Agricultural Society, Topsfield, Massachusetts

Makes about 4 dozen cookies

    1/2 cup shortening
    4 tablespoons (1/2 stick) butter, softened
    1 cup dark brown sugar (not packed)
    1 egg
    1/3 cup molasses
    11/2 teaspoons finely grated fresh ginger
    21/4 cups all-purpose flour, divided
    2 teaspoons baking soda
    1 teaspoon salt
    3/4 teaspoon ground cinnamon
    1/4 teaspoon ground cloves
    11/2 cups raisins
    1/4 teaspoon mace
    Granulated sugar

Beat the shortening and butter in a large bowl until creamy. Add the brown sugar, egg, molasses and ginger, beating until light and fluffy. Combine 2 cups of the flour, the baking soda, salt, cinnamon and cloves in a small bowl; gradually stir into the butter mixture. Dust the raisins with the remaining 1/4 cup flour and the mace; stir into the batter and mix well. Cover and refrigerate until the dough is firm enough to handle.

(continued)

Clockwise from left: Raisin-Spice Cookies, Old-Fashioned Peanut Brittle (page 173), Grand Marnier Brownies (page 156)

For even baking and browning of cookies, bake them in the center of the oven. If the heat distribution in your oven is uneven, turn the cookie sheet halfway through the baking time. Most cookies bake quickly and should be watched carefully to avoid overbaking. It is generally better to slightly underbake, rather than to overbake cookies.

Preheat the oven to 375°F. Grease cookie sheets. Roll the chilled dough into small balls; roll each ball in granulated sugar. Place about 1½ inches apart on the prepared cookie sheets. Bake for 10 minutes. Remove the cookies to wire racks to cool. Store in an airtight container.

San Shoppell
Boston, Massachusetts

GRAND MARNIER BROWNIES

♦ First place winner in the Topsfield Fair Baking Competition, sponsored by the Essex Agricultural Society, Topsfield, Massachusetts

Makes about 2 dozen brownies

   2 (1-ounce) squares unsweetened chocolate
   2 cups sugar
 ½ cup vegetable oil
 ½ cup Grand Marnier liqueur
 ¼ cup chocolate-flavored syrup
   4 eggs, beaten
   3 tablespoons unsweetened cocoa
   2 teaspoons grated orange rind
   1 teaspoon orange juice
1¼ cups all-purpose flour
   1 teaspoon baking powder
   1 (12-ounce) package semisweet chocolate chips, divided
   2 tablespoons shortening
     Fresh mint sprigs and orange rind, for garnish

Brownies are high on almost everyone's list of favorite foods. These dense, fudgelike chocolate squares are a cross between a cake and a cookie and have been around since the late nineteenth century. Ideally they are eaten with one in each hand and a glass of very cold milk on the side. The name "brownie" comes from their rich brown color.

Preheat the oven to 350°F. Grease a 13 × 9-inch pan. Melt the unsweetened chocolate in the top of a double boiler over hot, not boiling, water. Remove from the heat and mix in the sugar, oil, liqueur, syrup, eggs, cocoa and orange rind and juice. Stir in the flour, baking powder and 8 ounces of the chocolate chips. Spread the batter evenly in the prepared pan. Bake for 22 minutes.

As soon as the brownies are removed from the oven, melt the remaining 4 ounces chocolate chips and the shortening in the top of a double boiler over hot, not boiling, water; stir until smooth. Spread the hot chocolate mixture over the warm brownies. Cool completely in the pan on a wire rack. Cut into 2-inch squares. Garnish with mint and orange rind.

Mary P. Murphy
Hampton, New Hampshire

TROPICAL OAT SQUARES

♦ Silver Plate winner in Silver Oats, a Quaker Food Service program to benefit Second Harvest, America's Food Bank Network

Makes about 2 dozen squares

4 cups (8 ounces) Quaker® Oat Squares
4 cups (1 pound) Quaker® 100% Natural Cereal
2 cups sliced or slivered almonds, toasted
1¹/₂ cups chopped dried pineapple pieces
1¹/₂ cups sweetened shredded coconut, toasted
1¹/₂ cups dark raisins
1¹/₄ cups (2¹/₂ sticks) butter
1¹/₂ cups light brown sugar, lightly packed
³/₄ cup honey
1¹/₄ teaspoons ground ginger
¹/₂ cup nonfat dry milk powder

Lightly grease a 15¹/₂ × 10¹/₂ × 1-inch jelly-roll pan. Toss the cereals with the almonds, pineapple, coconut and raisins in a large bowl. Melt the butter in a medium-sized saucepan over low heat. Stir in the sugar, honey and ginger; simmer for 2 minutes. Remove the pan from the heat. Stir in the milk powder; mix thoroughly. Pour the sugar syrup over the cereal mixture in the bowl; toss well to coat. Spread the mixture evenly in the prepared pan, pressing down gently to make the mixture more compact. Cover the pan loosely and refrigerate for at least 1 hour. Cut into 2¹/₂-inch squares and serve chilled.

John T. Pence and Denise Wiseman
Kansas State University

Toasting Nuts

Spread the nuts on a baking sheet in a single layer and toast them in a preheated 350°F oven for 8 to 10 minutes or until very lightly browned. Use them immediately or store them in a covered container in the refrigerator.

PEANUT BLOSSOMS

◆ Finalist at the Pillsbury BAKE-OFF® Contest in Los Angeles, California

Makes about 4 dozen cookies

1³/₄ cups Pillsbury's BEST® All Purpose or Unbleached Flour
  ¹/₂ cup granulated sugar
  ¹/₂ cup packed brown sugar
  1 teaspoon baking soda
  ¹/₂ teaspoon salt
  ¹/₂ cup shortening
  ¹/₂ cup peanut butter
  2 tablespoons milk
  1 teaspoon vanilla extract
  1 egg
    Granulated sugar
  48 milk chocolate candy kisses, unwrapped

Preheat the oven to 375°F. Combine the flour, the ¹/₂ cup granulated sugar, the brown sugar, baking soda, salt, shortening, peanut butter, milk, vanilla and egg in a large bowl at low speed until a stiff dough forms. Shape into 1-inch balls; roll each ball in granulated sugar. Place the balls 2 inches apart on ungreased cookie sheets. Bake for 10 to 12 minutes or until golden brown. Remove the cookie sheets from the oven and immediately top each cookie with a chocolate kiss, pressing down firmly so the cookie cracks around the edge. Remove the cookies to wire racks to cool.

Mrs. Chester Smith
Gibsonburg, Ohio

𝓘t is an astonishing fact that if you ask most people what they like to eat when they are alone, they will unhesitatingly declare that it is peanut butter. By the last day of high school, the average student will have eaten 1500 peanut-butter-and-jelly sandwiches. And enough peanut butter is consumed annually by Americans of all ages to cover the floor of the Grand Canyon!

𝓤nbaked cookie dough can be refrigerated for up to two weeks or frozen up to six weeks. Label the dough with baking information for convenience.

Left to right: Tropical Oat Squares (page 157), Peanut Blossoms

You may be astonished to learn that a single banana contains nearly five teaspoons of sugar, almost twice as much as many of the popular candy bars. Even so, an average size banana only has eighty to ninety calories. Bananas also contain a hefty dose of the mineral potassium and are low in fat. You probably already know that bananas are one of the most frequently eaten of all fruits and are grown in the tropics. But did you know that they are grown on artificially heated soil in Iceland?

BRIDGET'S SOUR CREAM BANANA BARS

◆ First place in the Sour Cream Cookie category of the Culinary Department at the Kentucky State Fair, Louisville, Kentucky

Makes about 4 dozen bars

1¹/₂ cups granulated sugar
 1 cup sour cream
 ¹/₂ cup (1 stick) butter or margarine, softened
 2 eggs
1¹/₂ cups mashed bananas (about 3 large bananas)
 2 teaspoons vanilla extract
 2 cups all-purpose flour
 1 teaspoon salt
 1 teaspoon baking soda
 ¹/₂ cup chopped nuts
    Browned Butter Frosting (recipe follows)

Preheat the oven to 375°F. Grease and flour a 15¹/₂ × 10¹/₂ × 1-inch jelly-roll pan. Mix the granulated sugar, sour cream, butter and eggs in a medium-sized bowl; beat for 1 minute on low speed, scraping the bowl occasionally. Add the bananas and vanilla; beat for 30 seconds. Beat in the flour, salt and baking soda on medium speed for 1 minute, scraping the bowl occasionally. Stir in the nuts. Spread the batter evenly in the prepared pan. Bake for 20 to 25 minutes or until light brown. Cool completely in the pan on a wire rack. Frost with Browned Butter Frosting; cut into 2¹/₂ × 1¹/₂-inch bars.

BROWNED BUTTER FROSTING

    4 tablespoons (¹/₂ stick) butter or margarine
    2 cups powdered sugar
    1 teaspoon vanilla extract
    3 tablespoons milk

Heat the butter in a small heavy saucepan over medium heat until it turns a delicate brown. Remove from the heat and beat in the powdered sugar. Add the vanilla and milk; continue beating until the frosting is smooth and of a spreading consistency.

Robin Maxwell
Louisville, Kentucky

ARMENIAN KURABIA

♦ Prize winner in the Cookies category at the Michigan State Fair, Detroit, Michigan

Makes about 4 dozen cookies

   1 pound (4 sticks) butter, clarified
1½ cups sugar
   3 cups all-purpose flour

Cream the clarified butter with the sugar in an electric mixer until the mixture is thick and creamy and the sugar is no longer grainy. (This may take from 15 to 30 minutes, but is the most important step. The butter must be clarified.) Gradually beat in the flour. If necessary, cover and refrigerate the dough for easier handling.

Preheat the oven to 300°F. Shape the dough by hand into desired shapes and place 2 inches apart on cold, ungreased cookie sheets. (Or, place the dough into a pastry bag fitted with a large tip and press out into finger-shaped cookies.) Bake for 15 to 20 minutes or until the bottoms are very lightly browned. *Do not allow the tops to brown.* If the cookies are too fragile to remove from the cookie sheet, cool them slightly so they become fairly firm, then transfer to a wire rack.

Aimee Hachigian
Detroit, Michigan

In Armenia, where this recipe has been handed down through generations, a bride's worth was judged by the quality of her kurabia—it should literally melt in your mouth!

FAMILY FAVORITE COOKIES

♦ First place winner in the Cookies category at the National Date Festival, Indio, California

Makes 3 dozen cookies

1¾ cups all-purpose flour
   ½ teaspoon baking soda
   ¼ teaspoon salt
   ¼ teaspoon ground cinnamon
   ¼ teaspoon mace
   ¼ teaspoon ground cardamom
   8 tablespoons (1 stick) butter, softened
   1 cup packed brown sugar
   1 egg
   ¼ cup cold coffee
   1 pound fresh dates, pitted and chopped
   1 cup finely chopped pecans   *(continued)*

To easily shape drop cookies, use an ice cream scoop with a release bar. The bar usually has a number on it indicating the number of scoops that can be made from one quart of ice cream. The handiest sizes are a #80 or #90 scoop. These will yield about one rounded teaspoonful of dough for each cookie.

Preheat the oven to 350°F. Lightly grease 2 cookie sheets. Sift the flour with the baking soda, salt and spices. Cream the butter and sugar in a large bowl. Add the egg, beating until fluffy. Fold in the coffee, dates and pecans. Add the flour mixture, stirring to blend. Drop the dough by rounded teaspoonfuls 2 inches apart onto the prepared cookie sheets. Bake for 13 to 15 minutes or until lightly browned. Remove the cookies to wire racks to cool. When completely cooled, store them in an airtight container for a week or until their flavor mellows.

Mae M. Gruel
Escondido, California

OATMEAL CARMELITAS

♦ Finalist at the Pillsbury BAKE-OFF® Contest in Los Angeles, California

Makes 3 dozen bars

CRUST
   **2 cups Pillsbury's BEST® All Purpose or Unbleached
      Flour**
   2 cups quick-cooking rolled oats, uncooked
   1¹/₂ cups packed brown sugar
   1¹/₄ cups margarine or butter, softened
   1 teaspoon baking soda
   ¹/₂ teaspoon salt

FILLING
   1 cup (6 ounces) semisweet chocolate chips
   ¹/₂ cup chopped nuts
   1 (12-ounce) jar caramel ice cream topping (1 cup)
   3 tablespoons all-purpose or unbleached flour

Preheat the oven to 350°F. Grease a 13 × 9-inch pan. Combine all the crust ingredients in a large bowl; mix until crumbly. Press half of the crumb mixture, about 3 cups, into the bottom of the prepared pan; reserve the remaining crumb mixture. Bake for 10 minutes. Remove from the oven; sprinkle the chocolate chips and nuts over the warm crust. Combine the caramel topping and 3 tablespoons flour in a small bowl; drizzle evenly over the chips and nuts. Sprinkle with the reserved crumb mixture. Bake for an additional 18 to 22 minutes or until golden brown. Cool completely in the pan on a wire rack. Refrigerate for 1 to 2 hours, then cut into bars.

Mrs. Ronald Larson
Kennedy, Minnesota

Top to bottom: Family Favorite Cookies (page 161),
Oatmeal Carmelitas

*Because these
meringue treats are left
in the oven for eight to
twelve hours, you can
make them in the
evening and they will be
done by morning. Hence
the Howell family's
nickname for them—
"Go to Bed Cookies."*

CHOCOLATE CHIP & MINT ▸ MERINGUE COOKIES

♦ Prize winner in the Cookies category at the Michigan State Fair, Detroit, Michigan

Makes about 4 dozen cookies

3 egg whites
1/2 teaspoon cream of tartar
   Pinch of salt
3/4 cup sugar
4 drops green food coloring
4 drops mint extract
1 (6-ounce) package miniature chocolate chips

Preheat the oven to 375°F. Grease and lightly flour 2 cookie sheets. Beat the egg whites with the cream of tartar and salt until foamy. Gradually beat in the sugar, 2 tablespoons at a time, until the egg whites form soft peaks. Stir in the food coloring and mint extract, then gently fold in the chocolate chips. Drop the meringue by teaspoonfuls 1 inch apart onto the prepared cookie sheets. Place in the preheated oven, then turn off the heat and let sit in the oven for 8 to 12 hours.

Katherine Howell
Royal Oak, Michigan

PEANUT BUTTER AND OAT BARS

♦ Second place winner in the Cookies category in the Recipe Contest at the National Peanut Festival, Dothan, Alabama

Makes about 3 dozen bars

BARS
4 cups uncooked rolled oats
1 cup packed brown sugar
1/4 cup light corn syrup
2/3 cup (12/3 sticks) butter, melted
1/2 cup crunchy peanut butter
1 teaspoon vanilla extract

TOPPING
1 cup (6 ounces) semisweet chocolate chips
1 cup (6 ounces) peanut butter chips
2/3 cup crunchy peanut butter   *(continued)*

Preheat the oven to 400°F. Grease a 13 × 9-inch pan. To make the bars, combine the oats, sugar and corn syrup in a large bowl. Pour in the butter and mix well. Stir in the ¹/₂ cup peanut butter and vanilla. Pat the mixture evenly into the prepared pan. Bake for 12 minutes. Cool completely in the pan on a wire rack.

Combine all the topping ingredients in the top of a double boiler over hot, not boiling, water. Stir until the chips are completely melted. Spread the topping mixture over the oat bars. Cut into 2 × 1¹/₂-inch bars.

Note: These bars are better when made a day in advance of serving.

Reesa Byrd
Enterprise, Alabama

When a recipe calls for greasing the cookie sheets, use shortening or a nonstick cooking spray for best results. Or, use parchment paper instead of greasing. It eliminates cleanup, bakes the cookies more evenly and allows them to cool right on the paper instead of on wire racks.

FESTIVE & FRUITY PEANUT ▶ BUTTER COOKIES

♦ First place winner in the Cookies category at the National Peanut Festival, sponsored by the Alabama Peanut Producers Association, Wiregrass, Alabama

Makes about 2 dozen cookies

    3 cups all-purpose flour
 ¹/₂ teaspoon salt
 ¹/₂ teaspoon baking soda
    1 cup granulated sugar
    1 cup packed brown sugar
    1 cup raisins
    1 cup chunky applesauce
    1 cup shortening
    1 cup chunky peanut butter
 ¹/₄ cup finely chopped candied fruits
    2 eggs
    1 teaspoon vanilla extract
       Additional candied fruit, for decoration

Preheat the oven to 350°F. Lightly grease cookie sheets. Sift the flour with the salt and baking soda. Combine the remaining ingredients, *except* the additional candied fruit, in a large bowl; mix well. Stir in the flour mixture. Drop the dough by teaspoonfuls 2 inches apart onto the prepared cookie sheets. Bake for 10 to 15 minutes or until lightly browned. Remove the cookies to wire racks to cool. Decorate, if desired, with additional candied fruit.

Lillian Beebe
Dothan, Alabama

CRANBERRY CRUNCHIES

♦ First prize winner in the Cookies category in the Make It Better with Cranberries Contest, sponsored by the Cape Cod Cranberry Growers' Association, the Massachusetts Department of Food & Agriculture and Cranberry World Visitors Center, Plymouth, Massachusetts

Makes 2 dozen sandwich cookies

COOKIES
8 tablespoons (1 stick) butter
1 cup uncooked rolled oats
3/4 cup granulated sugar
3 tablespoons all-purpose flour
1 teaspoon baking powder
1/2 teaspoon salt
1 egg, lightly beaten

FILLING
8 tablespoons (1 stick) butter or margarine, softened
3 heaping tablespoons marshmallow creme
1 cup powdered sugar
1/2 teaspoon vanilla extract
   Milk, if needed
1 cup finely chopped fresh cranberries

Preheat the oven to 375°F. Grease and flour 2 cookie sheets. To make the cookies, melt 8 tablespoons butter in a medium-sized saucepan over low heat. Remove the pan from the heat and stir in the oats, granulated sugar, flour, baking powder, salt and egg. Let cool for 10 minutes. Drop the mixture by teaspoonfuls about 3 inches apart onto the prepared cookie sheets. Bake for 8 minutes. Immediately remove the cookies from the sheets to a wire rack to cool completely. If a cookie sticks to the sheet, return it to the oven for a minute or two, then try again.

To make the filling, beat the softened butter and marshmallow creme in a medium-sized bowl until fluffy. Beat in the powdered sugar and vanilla, adding milk, if needed, to thin. Stir in the cranberries. Spread the filling on the flat side of half of the cookies. Top with the remaining cookies, flat side down, forming sandwiches.

Lorraine Carr
Rochester, Massachusetts

CARAMELS

♦ Preliminary winner in the Candy category in the annual recipe contest sponsored by the *Reflector-Chronicle*, Abilene, Kansas

Makes about 1¹/₂ pounds

4 tablespoons (¹/₂ stick) butter
2 cups sugar
1 cup heavy cream
¹/₂ cup light corn syrup
¹/₂ cup milk
1 teaspoon vanilla extract

Grease an 8-inch square pan with a little of the butter. Combine all the ingredients *except* the vanilla in a medium-sized heavy saucepan. Cook over medium-high heat for about 30 minutes or until the mixture reaches the firm-ball stage (245°F) on a candy thermometer. Remove from the heat and stir in the vanilla. Pour the caramel mixture into the prepared pan. When almost cooled, cut into squares.

Virginia Romberger
Solomon, Kansas

CHOCONUTTER APPLES

♦ Shared honors in the seventh- to ninth-grade category in the Apple Recipe Contest for Grades 5 through 12, sponsored by *The Hartford Courant*, Hartford, Connecticut

Makes 8 pieces

4 (1-ounce) squares semisweet chocolate
³/₄ cup peanut butter
1 McIntosh apple, cored and cut into eighths

Melt the chocolate in the top of a double boiler over hot, not boiling, water. Stir until it is smooth and completely melted. Spread the peanut butter evenly over the apple slices and place on waxed paper. Spoon about ¹/₂ tablespoonful of melted chocolate over each apple slice. If some chocolate remains in the pan, spread it evenly over the 8 slices; cool.

Shane Donahue
Tolland, Connecticut

Testing Candy Mixtures

Sugar and water syrups are the foundations of many candies. Temperature is a guide as to when the syrup mixture has reached its proper stage. When other ingredients are added, the syrup may reach this stage at a different temperature. Therefore, test the consistency of a syrup by dropping a small amount of it into some ice water as it nears the target temperature. Following are descriptions of a few of the stages:

The syrup is at the "soft-ball" stage (234° to 240°F) if you can gather the cooled syrup into a very sticky ball that immediately loses its shape and flattens. At the "firm-ball" stage (244° to 248°F), you can mold the syrup into a ball that will retain its shape a little longer than the soft-ball. It will feel firm but still sticky. The "hard-crack" stage (300° to 310°F) is reached when the syrup solidifies in the water. It will snap easily when bent, have a yellowish appearance and will not be sticky.

NEVER-FAIL FUDGE ▸

◆ Overall winner in the Candy category in the Cooking Contest at the Louisiana Pecan Festival, Colfax, Louisiana

Makes about 1½ pounds

    2 cups sugar
    1 (6-ounce) can evaporated milk
   10 large marshmallows
    1 cup (6 ounces) semisweet chocolate chips
    1 cup chopped pecans
    8 tablespoons (1 stick) margarine, cut into pieces
    1 teaspoon vanilla extract

Thoroughly grease a 9-inch square pan. Combine the sugar, milk and marshmallows in a small saucepan. Slowly bring to a boil over medium heat; simmer for 6 minutes, stirring occasionally. Meanwhile, combine the chocolate chips, pecans, margarine and vanilla in a large bowl. Pour the hot marshmallow mixture into the bowl and stir with a wooden spoon until both the chips and margarine are completely melted. Pour the fudge mixture into the prepared pan and refrigerate until firm; cut into squares.

Shirley Parsons
Alexandria, Louisiana

If fudge is difficult to cut into neat squares, place it in the refrigerator or freezer until firm. This will make it easier to cut.

BLACK WALNUT FUDGE ▸

◆ Third place winner in the Black Walnut Bake Off at the Black Walnut Festival, Spencer, West Virginia

Makes about 3 pounds

    4 cups granulated sugar
    8 tablespoons (1 stick) margarine
    1 (12-ounce) can evaporated milk
    3 tablespoons light corn syrup
    1 pound high quality white chocolate,* broken into
        small pieces
    1 (13-ounce) jar marshmallow creme
    1 cup black walnuts
    1 tablespoon vanilla extract   *(continued)*

When it first started in 1954, the Black Walnut Baking Contest was a regional competition for the best recipes in eight counties of West Virginia. The county winners were then invited to prepare their dishes during a bake off at the annual Black Walnut Festival. Now, the contest has expanded into a major statewide competition.

*Do not use confectioner's coating or compound chocolate.

Grease a 13 × 9-inch pan. Combine the sugar, margarine, milk and corn syrup in a large saucepan. Cook over medium heat, stirring until the sugar dissolves. Stop stirring and continue heating until the mixture reaches the soft-ball stage (234°F) on a candy thermometer. Remove from the heat and stir in the white chocolate, marshmallow creme, walnuts and vanilla, beating well after each addition. Pour into the prepared pan and set aside to cool. Refrigerate until chilled, then cut into pieces.

Una Belle Waskey
Sandyville, West Virginia

CHOCOLATE & PEANUT BUTTER SQUARES

♦ First place winner in the Candy category in the annual recipe contest sponsored by the *Reflector-Chronicle*, Abilene, Kansas

Makes about 2 dozen squares

   1 cup peanut butter
   1 cup (6 ounces) semisweet chocolate chips
   8 tablespoons (1 stick) butter or margarine, cut into
      small pieces
   1 (10¹/₂-ounce) package miniature marshmallows
   2 cups crispy rice cereal

Coat an 8-inch square pan with nonstick cooking spray. Heat the peanut butter, chocolate chips and butter in a 3-quart saucepan over low heat until the butter and the chocolate chips melt; stir until smooth. Stir in the marshmallows. Heat for 1 minute or until the marshmallows are slightly melted. Stir in the cereal until well blended. Spread the mixture evenly in the prepared pan. Cover and refrigerate for 2 to 3 hours or until firm. Cut into 1¹/₂-inch squares.

Peggy Meuli
Hope, Kansas

OLD-FASHIONED PEANUT BRITTLE

♦ Third place winner in the Candies category in the Recipe Contest at the National Peanut Festival, Dothan, Alabama

Makes about 1 pound

1 cup sugar
1 cup light corn syrup
1 cup raw peanuts
1 teaspoon baking soda
1 teaspoon butter

Grease a baking sheet. Place the sugar and corn syrup in a medium-sized heavy saucepan. Bring to a full boil over high heat. Add the peanuts and cook until the mixture reaches the hard-crack stage (302°F) on a candy thermometer. Remove the pan from the heat and stir in the baking soda and butter. Spread the mixture on the prepared baking sheet and cool. When cooled, break the brittle into bite-sized pieces.

Anne Dawsey
Dothan, Alabama

Peanut brittle has been around since the turn of the nineteenth century. It is made by adding raw peanuts to a syrup of boiling water and sugar. The molten mass is spread onto a greased baking sheet and left to harden. It is then broken into random shapes. To keep it brittle, store it in an airtight container, layering it between pieces of waxed paper.

BOURBON BALLS

♦ First place in the Candy category of the Culinary Department at the Kentucky State Fair, Louisville, Kentucky

Makes about 1 pound

1 cup crushed vanilla wafers
1 cup finely chopped walnuts
1 cup powdered sugar
1/4 cup bourbon whiskey
2 tablespoons unsweetened cocoa
1 1/2 tablespoons light corn syrup
    Additional powdered sugar

Combine the crushed wafers, the walnuts, 1 cup powdered sugar, the bourbon, cocoa and corn syrup in a medium-sized bowl. Dust hands with powdered sugar and roll the mixture into small balls. Roll each ball in powdered sugar. Store in a cool place until ready to serve.

Lynn McCoy
Louisville, Kentucky

PIES

CARAMELIZED GINGERSNAP PEAR TART

♦ Winner in the Philly "Hall of Fame" Recipe Contest, sponsored by Philadelphia Brand® Cream Cheese

Makes 6 to 8 servings

1½ cups gingersnap cookie crumbs
½ cup finely chopped nuts
⅓ cup (⅔ stick) margarine, melted
2 (8-ounce) packages cream cheese, softened
¼ cup granulated sugar
2 tablespoons pear nectar or pear brandy
½ teaspoon vanilla extract
3 ripe pears*
¼ cup packed dark brown sugar
¼ teaspoon ground ginger

Preheat the oven to 350°F. Combine the cookie crumbs, nuts and margarine in a small bowl. Press onto the bottom and up the side of a 10-inch quiche dish or 9-inch pie plate. Bake for 5 minutes; set aside to cool.

Combine the cream cheese and granulated sugar, mixing at medium speed until well blended. Blend in the nectar and vanilla. Pour the cheese mixture over the prepared crust. Cover; refrigerate for several hours or overnight.

When ready to serve, heat the broiler. Pare and thinly slice the pears. Arrange the pear slices on top of the cream cheese mixture. Combine the brown sugar and ginger; sprinkle over the pears. Broil for 3 to 5 minutes or until the sugar is melted and bubbly. Serve at once.

You can substitute 1 (16-ounce) can pear halves, drained and thinly sliced, for the fresh pears.

Jane Exline
Milwaukee, Wisconsin

MY GOLDEN HARVEST APPLE PIE

♦ First prize winner in the New England Best Two-Crusted Apple Pie Contest at the Salem Cross Inn, West Brookfield, Massachusetts

Makes one 9-inch pie

CRUST
  2 cups all-purpose flour
  1/2 teaspoon salt
  2/3 cup shortening
  4 to 5 tablespoons ice water
  1 1/2 teaspoons all-purpose flour

FILLING
  2 1/2 cups thinly sliced Golden Delicious apples
  2 1/2 cups thinly sliced Stayman apples
  1/2 cup sugar*
  1 to 2 tablespoons all-fruit orange marmalade
  1 teaspoon ground cinnamon
  1 teaspoon ground nutmeg
  1 tablespoon all-purpose flour
  2 tablespoons margarine

  2 tablespoons skim milk

Preheat the oven to 450°F. To make the crust, combine the 2 cups flour and the salt in a medium-sized bowl. Cut in the shortening until the mixture is crumbly. Sprinkle the ice water, 1 tablespoon at a time, over the flour mixture and toss lightly. Add just enough water to make the mixture begin to hold together. Form the pastry into a ball; divide in half. Roll each half out on a lightly floured surface into a 10-inch circle. Fit 1 circle into a 9-inch pie plate; sprinkle with the 1 1/2 teaspoons flour.

To make the filling, combine the apple slices, sugar, marmalade, spices and the 1 tablespoon flour in a large bowl; toss lightly. Mound the filling in the prepared crust and dot with the margarine. Place the second pastry circle over the filling; pinch and flute the edge to seal. Brush the top crust with milk and use a knife to cut steam vents. Bake for 15 minutes. *Reduce the oven temperature to 375°F.* Continue baking for 30 to 35 minutes or until the crust is golden brown. Cool the pie on a wire rack.

*Less sugar may be used depending on the sweetness of the apples.

Charlotte Granville
Manchester, Connecticut

CRANBERRY-RHUBARB PIE

♦ Second prize winner in the Pies category in the Make It Better with Cranberries Contest, sponsored by the Cape Cod Cranberry Growers' Association, the Massachusetts Department of Food & Agriculture and Cranberry World Visitors Center, Plymouth, Massachusetts

Makes one 9-inch pie

> **Pastry dough for a 9-inch double-crust pie**
> **3 eggs, lightly beaten**
> **1¹/₂ cups granulated sugar**
> **¹/₄ cup milk or cream (optional)**
> **¹/₄ cup all-purpose flour**
> **¹/₄ teaspoon ground cinnamon**
> **¹/₄ teaspoon ground nutmeg**
> **Dash of salt**
> **2 cups finely chopped fresh cranberries**
> **2 cups finely chopped rhubarb**
> **1 tablespoon butter or margarine**
> **1 tablespoon milk**
> **Powdered sugar (optional)**

Preheat the oven to 350°F. Line a 9-inch pie plate with half of the pastry; reserve the other half to make a lattice top. Combine the eggs, granulated sugar, the ¹/₄ cup milk, flour, spices and salt in a large bowl. Stir in the cranberries and rhubarb. Pour the filling into the pie shell and dot with the butter.

Roll out the remaining pastry and cut into long, ³/₄-inch-wide strips. Arrange the strips over the filling, weaving them over and under to make a lattice top. Combine the 1 tablespoon milk with any juice remaining in the large bowl; brush over the crust. Bake for 50 to 60 minutes or until golden brown. Cool the pie completely on a wire rack. Sprinkle with powdered sugar and refrigerate. Serve with whipped cream or ice cream.

Bernard Lacouture
Cataumet, Massachusetts

OREGON BLACKBERRY PIE

♦ Prize-winning recipe at the March of Dimes Gourmet Gala in Portland, Oregon

Makes one 9-inch pie

CRUST
  4 cups all-purpose flour
  1 teaspoon baking powder
  1 teaspoon salt
  1 teaspoon sugar
  1 cup shortening, chilled
  3/4 cup (1 1/2 sticks) butter
  1 tablespoon vinegar
    Ice water

FILLING
3 1/2 cups blackberries
  2/3 to 1 cup sugar (depending on the berries' sweetness)
  2 tablespoons cornstarch
  1 tablespoon lemon juice
  1/4 teaspoon ground cinnamon
  2 tablespoons butter

The blackberry is often called a bramble berry because it grows on thorny shrubs or brambles. Like raspberries, blackberries are extremely fragile and it is only recently that improved transportation methods have enabled them to become readily available. Their peak months are June, July and August. In addition to making a wonderful pie, blackberries combine beautifully with other berries for a fruit salad. Or, puree and strain them, then stir in a little sugar and you will have a splendid sauce for ice cream.

Preheat the oven to 425°F. To make the crust, sift the flour, baking powder, salt and 1 teaspoon sugar into a large bowl. Cut in the shortening and 3/4 cup butter until the mixture is crumbly. Place the vinegar in a measuring cup and add enough ice water to make 1/2 cup liquid. Add the liquid to the flour mixture; stir just until the mixture begins to hold together. Form the pastry into a ball. Divide in half; reserve one half for another use.* Roll out the other half on a lightly floured surface into a 10-inch circle. Fit the circle into a 9-inch pie plate; flute the edge.

To make the filling, combine the blackberries, 2/3 to 1 cup sugar, the cornstarch, lemon juice and cinnamon in a large bowl; mix thoroughly. Mound the filling in the prepared crust and dot with the 2 tablespoons butter. Bake for 15 minutes. *Reduce the oven temperature to 375°F.* Continue baking for 45 minutes. Cool the pie on a wire rack; serve warm or at room temperature.

The other half of the pastry can be rolled out to make a top crust for this pie. Or, make a double batch of filling and assemble two single-crust pies.

Francie Stevenson and Senator Robert Packwood

BUTTERMILK APPLE TART

♦ Shared honors in the seventh- to ninth-grade category in the Apple Recipe Contest for Grades 5 through 12, sponsored by *The Hartford Courant*, Hartford, Connecticut

Makes one 9-inch tart

     2 medium-size Granny Smith apples
     3 eggs
1¹/₂ cups sugar, divided
     1 cup buttermilk
 ¹/₃ cup (²/₃ stick) margarine or butter, melted
     2 tablespoons all-purpose flour
     2 teaspoons vanilla extract
     1 tablespoon ground cinnamon, divided
     2 teaspoons ground nutmeg, divided
     1 (9-inch) unbaked pie shell

Preheat the oven to 350°F. Pare and core the apples; cut into small chunks. Place them in a bowl; cover with cold water and set aside. Beat the eggs briefly at low speed until mixed. Add all but 1 teaspoon of the sugar, the buttermilk, margarine, flour, vanilla, 2 teaspoons of the cinnamon and 1¹/₂ teaspoons of the nutmeg; mix at low speed until well blended. Drain the apples thoroughly and place in the unbaked pie shell. Pour the buttermilk mixture over them. Combine the remaining 1 teaspoon sugar, 1 teaspoon cinnamon and ¹/₂ teaspoon nutmeg; sprinkle over the top. Bake for 50 to 60 minutes. Serve warm or at room temperature for the best flavor. Store in the refrigerator.

Matthew De Smith
West Simsbury, Connecticut

Tips for Making Pie Crusts

1. **Handle the pastry dough quickly and lightly; overworking it will make it tough.**

2. **The amount of liquid needed will vary depending on the type of flour and the humidity; the dough should be just moist enough to hold together.**

3. **If the dough is difficult to handle, refrigerate it until firm. (It can also be frozen; thaw in the refrigerator before rolling.)**

4. **Flour the rolling pin and surface just enough to prevent sticking. Too much flour worked into the dough will make it tough.**

5. **Handle the dough gently when transferring it to the pie plate. Pulling and stretching the dough will cause it to shrink during baking.**

Right after she won the Planters® Holiday Baking Contest, Bobbie Meyer found herself facing a microphone. "Entering the contest was as natural as breathing," she declared to all the world. We hope she took an extra-deep breath when she pocketed her grand prize of $100,000. "Nuts give recipes a rich taste," she said. She could say that again!

BERRY NUTTY PIE

♦ Winner of the Planters® Holiday Baking Contest, sponsored by Planters LifeSavers Co.

Makes 8 servings

   3 egg whites, at room temperature
3/4 cup granulated sugar
1/2 teaspoon baking powder
3/4 cup semisweet chocolate chips, divided
1/2 cup Planters® Pecan Pieces, divided
   1 cup crushed butter-flavored crackers
   1 teaspoon almond extract
   1 cup heavy cream
   2 tablespoons powdered sugar
1/2 teaspoon vanilla extract
   1 pint strawberries, hulled and sliced, divided

Preheat the oven to 350°F. Grease a 9-inch pie plate. Beat the egg whites in a small deep bowl until soft peaks form. Combine the granulated sugar and baking powder; gradually add to the egg whites, beating until stiff peaks form. Reserve 2 tablespoons of the chocolate chips; coarsely chop the remaining chips. Reserve 2 tablespoons of the pecans; grind the remaining pecans. Combine the cracker crumbs with the chopped chocolate chips and ground pecans in a small bowl; fold into the egg whites along with the almond extract. Spread the egg white mixture in the prepared pie plate. Bake for 25 minutes. Cool completely on a wire rack.

Beat the cream with the powdered sugar and vanilla in a small deep bowl until stiff. Reserve 3/4 cup of the strawberry slices for decoration; fold the remaining berries into the whipped cream. Spread the strawberry cream over the cooled baked layer. Decorate the pie with the reserved strawberries, pecans and chocolate chips.

Bobbie C. Meyer
Chauvin, Louisiana

Lemons contribute much to cooking. Besides their popular usage in lemonade and pies, lemons add flavor and zest to vegetables, fish and poultry. Lemon juice is a key ingredient in many salad dressings and marinades and also prevents other fruits, such as apples and bananas, from turning brown when sliced. A medium-size lemon will yield about 3 to 4 tablespoons of juice and 1 to 2 teaspoons of grated rind. If only a small amount of juice is needed, make a hole in the lemon with a toothpick. Squeeze out the amount you need, then seal the hole by inserting the toothpick in it; store in the refrigerator.

HEAVENLY SINFUL LEMON CHIFFON PIE

♦ Second place winner in the Junior division of the Citrus Pie Contest at the National Orange Show, San Bernardino, California

Makes one 9-inch pie

CRUST
1 cup all-purpose flour
1/4 cup sugar
1 tablespoon grated lemon rind
8 tablespoons (1 stick) butter
1 egg yolk, lightly beaten
1/2 teaspoon vanilla extract
1 teaspoon lemon juice

FILLING
4 eggs, separated*
1 cup sugar, divided
1/3 cup lemon juice
2 tablespoons grated lemon rind
1/2 teaspoon unflavored gelatine
1/4 teaspoon salt

Whipped cream and lemon pieces, for decorating

Preheat the oven to 400°F. To make the crust, combine the flour, 1/4 cup sugar and 1 tablespoon lemon rind in a medium-sized bowl. Cut in the butter until the mixture looks like coarse cornmeal. Stir in the egg yolk, vanilla and 1 teaspoon lemon juice. Press the mixture evenly into a 9-inch pie plate, leaving a small edge around the rim; prick the crust with a fork. Bake for 10 minutes; set aside to cool.

To make the filling, beat the egg yolks in a small bowl. Combine them with 1/2 cup of the sugar, 1/3 cup lemon juice, 2 tablespoons lemon rind and the gelatine in the top of a double boiler. Cook over boiling water, stirring constantly, for 5 minutes. Remove from the heat. Beat the egg whites with the salt in a large bowl until soft peaks form. Gradually add the remaining 1/2 cup sugar, beating until stiff. Fold the egg white mixture into the lemon mixture; pour into the prepared crust. Refrigerate until the filling is set. Decorate with whipped cream and lemon pieces.

Use clean, uncracked eggs.

Toni Canfill

"JUST IN CASE" PIE

♦ First place in the Chocolate Baked Goods category in the Chocolate Recipe Contest, sponsored by Lexington Market, Inc., Baltimore, Maryland

Makes about 8 servings

> Chocolate-Pecan Crust (recipe follows)
> 1 envelope unflavored gelatine
> 1/4 cup cold water
> 2 cups heavy cream, divided
> 1 cup (6 ounces) semisweet chocolate chips
> 2 eggs*
> 1 teaspoon vanilla extract
> 1 cup caramels (about 24)
> 2 tablespoons butter

Prepare the Chocolate-Pecan Crust. Sprinkle the gelatine over the water in a small saucepan; let stand 1 minute. Stir over low heat until the gelatine is completely dissolved, about 3 minutes. Stir in 1 cup of the cream. Heat just to a boil, then immediately pour into a food processor or blender. Add the chocolate chips and process until the chocolate is completely melted, about 1 minute. While processing, add 1/2 cup of the cream, the eggs and vanilla; continue processing until blended. Pour the chocolate mixture into a large bowl; refrigerate for about 15 minutes or until thickened.

Meanwhile, combine the caramels, 1/4 cup of the cream and the butter in a small saucepan. Heat over low heat, stirring occasionally, until the caramels are completely melted and the mixture is smooth. Pour over the prepared crust to cover the bottom; let stand at room temperature to cool for about 10 minutes.

Using a wire whisk, beat the thickened chocolate mixture until smooth. Pour over the caramel in the crust; refrigerate for about 3 hours or until firm. Whip the remaining 1/4 cup cream; use to decorate the pie.

Use clean, uncracked eggs.

CHOCOLATE-PECAN CRUST: Preheat the oven to 350°F. Combine 2 cups chocolate wafer cookie crumbs, 3/4 cup finely chopped pecans and 8 tablespoons (1 stick) melted butter or margarine in a small bowl. Press the mixture onto the bottom and up the side of a 9-inch deep-dish pie plate, forming a high rim. Bake for 10 minutes. Cool completely on a wire rack before filling.

Christa I. Schmitt
Sykesville, Maryland

Dissolving Gelatine

Gelatine is a wonderful ingredient, but is often considered difficult to use. A common cause of mishaps is adding the gelatine to a mixture before it is completely dissolved. Here is one foolproof method for dissolving gelatine successfully:

Sprinkle one package of gelatine over 1/4 cup of cold liquid in a small saucepan. Let it stand for 1 minute to soften and swell. Place the pan over low heat and stir until the gelatine is completely dissolved, about 3 minutes. Run a finger over the spoon to test for undissolved granules. If it is smooth to the touch, the gelatine is completely dissolved; if it feels grainy, continue heating until it feels smooth.

CAKES

EXOTIC DATE-CARROT CAKE

♦ Second place winner in the Cakes category at the National Date Festival, Indio, California

Makes 1 cake

2 cups chopped pitted dates
1 cup very hot water
1 cup vegetable oil
1 cup granulated sugar
3 eggs at room temperature, lightly beaten
2 cups finely grated carrots
1 cup crushed pineapple, drained with juice reserved
    for frosting
2 teaspoons vanilla extract
2¹/₂ cups all-purpose flour
1¹/₂ teaspoons baking powder
1 teaspoon baking soda
1 teaspoon salt
1¹/₂ teaspoons ground cinnamon
¹/₂ teaspoon ground nutmeg
¹/₂ cup chopped nuts
    Exotic Cream Cheese Frosting (recipe follows)

Preheat the oven to 350°F. Grease 2 (10-inch) round cake pans. Soak the dates in the hot water in a large bowl until softened, then mix to get a lumpy paste. Mix in the oil, granulated sugar and eggs. Stir in the carrots, pineapple and vanilla. Combine the flour, baking powder, baking soda, salt, cinnamon and nutmeg in a small bowl; stir into the date mixture. Add the nuts and

(continued)

Top to bottom: Exotic Date-Carrot Cake,
Supreme Chocolate Cheesecake (page 201)

mix well. Divide the batter evenly between the prepared pans. Bake for 40 to 45 minutes or until a toothpick inserted into the center comes out clean. Cool the layers in the pans on wire racks for 15 minutes. Loosen the edges and remove to the racks to cool completely. Fill and frost the layers with Exotic Cream Cheese Frosting.

EXOTIC CREAM CHEESE FROSTING: Cream 1 (8-ounce) package softened cream cheese and 8 tablespoons (1 stick) softened margarine in a large bowl. Stir in 2 teaspoons vanilla extract and 1 tablespoon reserved pineapple juice. Gradually add 4 cups powdered sugar and 1/2 teaspoon salt; mix well.

Note: For a more exotic texture, add 1 cup flaked coconut and 1 cup chopped nuts to the frosting.

Dianne Whitener
Thermal, California

PRUNE CAKE

♦ First prize winner in a Baking Contest sponsored by WCAX Radio, Burlington, Vermont

Makes 1 loaf

   1 (12-ounce) package pitted prunes
   3/4 cup boiling water
   1/2 cup vegetable oil
   1 teaspoon baking soda
   2 eggs
   1 cup sugar
   2 cups all-purpose flour
   1/2 cup chopped nuts

Preheat the oven to 350°F. Grease a 9 × 5 × 3-inch loaf pan. Combine the prunes, boiling water, oil and baking soda in a medium-sized bowl; let stand for 15 minutes. Beat the eggs with the sugar in a large bowl. Gradually stir in the flour. Add the prune mixture and mix well. Stir in the nuts. Pour the batter into the prepared pan. Bake for 1 hour or until a toothpick inserted into the center comes out clean. Cool the loaf in the pan on a wire rack for about 10 minutes. Loosen the edges and remove to the rack to cool completely.

Sadie Berinsky
Boston, Massachusetts

ZUCCHINI CAKE

♦ First prize winner at the Common Ground Fair, Windsor, Maine

Makes 2 loaves

2 cups all-purpose flour
2 teaspoons baking soda
2 teaspoons ground cinnamon
1 teaspoon salt
$1/4$ teaspoon baking powder
3 eggs
$1^1/2$ cups sugar
1 cup vegetable oil
1 teaspoon vanilla extract
2 cups grated zucchini
$1/2$ cup chopped walnuts (optional)
$1/2$ cup raisins (optional)

Preheat the oven to 350°F. Grease 2 ($8^1/2 \times 4^1/2 \times 2^1/2$-inch) loaf pans. Combine the flour, baking soda, cinnamon, salt and baking powder in a small bowl. Beat the eggs in a large bowl. Add the sugar, oil and vanilla, then stir in the flour mixture. Stir in the zucchini and mix well. Add the nuts and raisins; stir until thoroughly mixed. Divide the batter evenly between the prepared pans. Bake for 1 hour or until a toothpick inserted into the center comes out clean. Cool the loaves in the pans on wire racks for about 10 minutes. Loosen the edges and remove to the racks to cool completely.

Helene Berinsky
North Whitefield, Maine

Be sure to use the pan sizes specified in cake recipes. If the pan is too large, the cake will bake too quickly resulting in an overcooked bottom, pale top and coarse texture. If the pan is too small, the cake may spill over in the oven, causing not only a mess but a sunken middle as well.

CHOCOLATE PRALINE LAYER CAKE

New Orleans is the city most famous for its pralines, intensely sweet candies made from chopped nuts, preferably pecans, that are cooked in a light brown sugar syrup and formed into patties. This confection is named after César du Plessis-Praslin, whose chef created them in France in the late 1500s.

♦ Grand Prize winner at the Pillsbury BAKE-OFF® Contest in San Diego, California

Makes 12 servings

CAKE
8 tablespoons (1 stick) butter or margarine
1/4 cup heavy cream
1 cup packed brown sugar
3/4 cup coarsely chopped pecans
1 (16-ounce) package Pillsbury Plus Devil's Food Cake Mix
11/4 cups water
1/3 cup vegetable oil
3 eggs

TOPPING
13/4 cups heavy cream
1/4 cup powdered sugar
1/4 teaspoon vanilla extract

Pecan halves, for decoration
Chocolate curls, for decoration

Preheat the oven to 325°F. To make the cake, combine the butter, 1/4 cup cream and the brown sugar in a small heavy saucepan. Cook over low heat just until the butter is melted, stirring occasionally. Pour into 2 (8- or 9-inch) round cake pans and sprinkle evenly with the chopped pecans. Combine the cake mix, water, oil and eggs in a large bowl; beat at low speed until moistened, then beat at high speed for 2 minutes. Carefully spoon the batter over the pecan praline mixture in the pans. Bake for 35 to 45 minutes or until the cake springs back when touched lightly in the center. Cool the layers in the pans for 5 minutes, then remove from the pans to wire racks to cool completely.

To make the topping, beat the 13/4 cups cream in a small bowl until soft peaks form. Blend in the powdered sugar and vanilla and beat until stiff peaks form. To assemble the cake, place 1 layer on a serving plate, praline side up. Spread with half of the whipped cream. Top with the second layer, praline side up; spread the remaining whipped cream on top. Decorate with pecan halves and chocolate curls. Store in the refrigerator.

Julie Konecne
Bemidji, Minnesota

ORANGE CAKE

♦ First place winner in the Junior division of the Citrus Cake Contest at the National Orange Show, San Bernardino, California

Makes 1 cake

2 cups all-purpose flour
2¹/₂ teaspoons baking powder
¹/₄ teaspoon baking soda
¹/₄ teaspoon salt
8 tablespoons (1 stick) butter, softened
1 cup granulated sugar
¹/₂ cup chopped walnuts
1 tablespoon grated orange rind
¹/₄ cup orange juice
2 eggs
³/₄ cup mayonnaise
Orange Cream Frosting (recipe follows)
Orange peel, mint leaves and mandarin oranges, for decoration

Preheat the oven to 375°F. Grease a 13 × 9 × 2-inch pan. Sift the flour with the baking powder, baking soda and salt. Cream the butter and granulated sugar in a large bowl until light and fluffy. Stir in the walnuts, orange rind and juice; mix well. Add the eggs, one at a time, beating well after each addition. Add the dry ingredients alternately with the mayonnaise, stirring until smooth. Pour the batter into the prepared pan. Bake for 35 to 40 minutes or until a toothpick inserted into the center comes out clean. Cool the cake completely in the pan on a wire rack. Frost with Orange Cream Frosting and decorate with orange peel, mint leaves and mandarin oranges.

ORANGE CREAM FROSTING: Cream 3 tablespoons softened butter and 1 (3-ounce) package softened cream cheese with ¹/₄ cup orange juice and a dash of salt in a medium-sized bowl until light and fluffy. Gradually add 4¹/₂ cups sifted powdered sugar, beating until smooth.

Carrie Rogers
Hesperia, California

SOUR-CREAM COFFEE-CAKE CUPCAKES

♦ First place winner in the Cupcakes category in the Black Walnut Bake Off at the Black Walnut Festival, Spencer, West Virginia

Makes about 1¹/₂ dozen cupcakes

> 1 cup (2 sticks) butter, softened (do not use margarine)
> 2 cups plus 4 teaspoons granulated sugar, divided
> 2 eggs
> 1 cup sour cream
> 1 teaspoon vanilla extract
> 2 cups all-purpose flour
> ¹/₂ teaspoon baking soda
> 1 teaspoon salt
> 1 cup chopped black walnuts
> 1 teaspoon ground cinnamon

Preheat the oven to 350°F. Insert paper liners into 12 (2¹/₂-inch) muffin cups. Cream the butter in a large bowl. Gradually add the 2 cups granulated sugar, beating until light and fluffy. Beat in the eggs, one at a time. Fold in the sour cream and vanilla. Sift the flour with the baking soda and salt; fold into the butter mixture. Combine the 4 teaspoons granulated sugar, the walnuts and cinnamon in a small bowl; mix thoroughly.

Fill the prepared muffin cups one-third full with the batter. Sprinkle with two thirds of the nut mixture. Fill the cups with the remaining batter and sprinkle with the remaining nut mixture. Bake for 25 to 30 minutes or until golden brown and a toothpick inserted into the center comes out clean. Remove the cupcakes from the pan and cool on a wire rack.

Marie Bailey
Spencer, West Virginia

MÉGÈVE CAKE

♦ Third place in the Chocolate Baked Goods category in the Chocolate Recipe Contest, sponsored by Lexington Market, Inc., Baltimore, Maryland

Makes about 12 servings

MERINGUE
   3 egg whites
   1 cup minus 1 tablespoon superfine sugar

CHOCOLATE FILLING
   ²/₃ cup heavy cream
   7 squares (7 ounces) semisweet chocolate, cut into
      small pieces
3¹/₂ squares (3¹/₂ ounces) unsweetened chocolate, cut into
      small pieces
   4 tablespoons (¹/₂ stick) butter or margarine
   4 egg whites
   1 cup minus 1 tablespoon superfine sugar
   1 teaspoon vanilla extract

   Chocolate curls, for decorating
   Powdered sugar, for decorating

Grease 1 large and 1 small baking sheet. Dust lightly with flour and tap off the excess. Using an 8-inch round cake pan as a guide, draw 2 circles on the large baking sheet and 1 on the small sheet. Preheat the oven to 300°F.

To make the meringue, beat the 3 egg whites in a large bowl until foamy and doubled in volume. Beat in the superfine sugar, 1 tablespoon at a time, until stiff peaks form. Spoon the mixture evenly onto the 3 circles on the baking sheets and spread out to the edges of each one. Bake for 30 minutes or until the layers are firm and lightly golden. Cool 5 minutes on the baking sheets on wire racks, then loosen the layers carefully with a wide spatula and slide them onto the racks; cool completely.

To make the filling, heat the cream in the top of a double boiler over hot water; add the chocolates. Continue to heat, stirring often with a wooden spoon, until the chocolate is completely melted. Stir in the butter until melted; remove from the heat. Beat the 4 egg whites in a large bowl until foamy and doubled in volume. Beat in the superfine sugar, 1 tablespoon at a time, until stiff peaks form. Partially fill the bottom of the double boiler with ice and water. Set the chocolate mixture over the ice

(continued)

Making Chocolate Curls

Melt 7 (1-ounce) squares of semisweet chocolate in a small bowl over hot water, stirring often. Pour the melted chocolate onto a cold baking sheet and spread out into a 6×4-inch rectangle. Refrigerate just until set, about 15 minutes. Pull the long edge of a long metal spatula across the surface of the soft chocolate, letting it curl up in front of the spatula. Place the curls on waxed paper. Repeat this process to make enough curls to decorate an 8- or 9-inch cake.

water and beat until light, fluffy and almost doubled in volume, scraping down the side of the pan often. Gently fold the chocolate into the egg white mixture until no streaks of white or brown remain. Fold in the vanilla.

Place 1 baked meringue layer on a serving plate and spread with about 1 cup of the chocolate filling. Top with another layer and 1/2 cup filling. Place the third layer on top and frost the side and top with the remaining filling. Place chocolate curls around the side and pile high on top of the cake; refrigerate. Thirty minutes before serving, remove the cake from the refrigerator to soften it and make cutting easier. Sprinkle powdered sugar over the top. Cut into wedges with a sharp, serrated knife.

Jill Earl
Baltimore, Maryland

For the best angel food cake ever, follow these tips:

1. *Always use cake flour.*

2. *Don't underbeat the egg whites; be sure to beat them into stiff peaks.*

3. *Use a totally grease-free cake pan. To ensure that your pan has no film of grease, never use it to bake anything but angel food cakes.*

ANGEL FOOD CAKE ▶

♦ Prize winner in the Cakes category at the Michigan State Fair, Detroit, Michigan

Makes 1 cake

1¼ cups cake flour, sifted
1⅓ cups plus 1/2 cup sugar, divided
 12 egg whites
1¼ teaspoons cream of tartar
 1/4 teaspoon salt
  1 teaspoon vanilla extract
 1/4 teaspoon almond extract
     Fresh strawberries, for serving

Preheat the oven to 350°F. Sift the cake flour with the 1/2 cup sugar 4 times. Beat the egg whites with the cream of tartar, salt and flavorings in a large bowl until stiff peaks form. Add the remaining 1⅓ cups sugar in 4 additions, beating after each addition. Fold in the flour mixture with a large spoon. Pour the mixture into an ungreased 10-inch tube pan. Bake for 35 to 40 minutes. Invert the pan and allow the cake to cool completely before removing it from the pan. Serve with fresh strawberries.

Nancy Turner
St. Clair Shores, Michigan

PINEAPPLE MACADAMIA CHEESEPIE

The marvelous macadamia nut is second to none for its buttery smooth flavor and delectable crunch. It is the world's most expensive nut and considered by many to also be the world's finest. Native to Australia, the macadamia tree was named after the man who cultivated it, chemist John MacAdam. It was brought to Hawaii in the late nineteenth century and has since become the state's third-largest crop.

♦ Grand Prize/first prize winner in the Dessert category in "Generations of Good Cooking," an employee contest sponsored by Dole Packaged Foods Company

Makes 6 servings

CRUST
   1 cup chopped macadamia nuts
   3/4 cup graham cracker crumbs
   6 tablespoons (3/4 stick) butter, melted
   2 tablespoons sugar

FILLING
   1 (8-ounce) can Dole® Crushed Pineapple in Juice
   12 ounces cream cheese, softened
   1 egg
   3/4 cup plain yogurt
   1/2 cup sugar
   1 teaspoon vanilla extract

Combine all the crust ingredients in a small bowl. Press onto the bottom and up the side of an 8-inch pie plate; refrigerate.

Preheat the oven to 350°F. Drain the pineapple well, pressing out the excess juice with the back of a spoon. Combine the cream cheese, egg, yogurt, sugar and vanilla in a medium-sized bowl and blend thoroughly. Spread all but 2 tablespoons of the pineapple over the prepared crust. Pour the cheese filling over the pineapple. Bake for 20 minutes. Cool the pie completely on a wire rack, then refrigerate for at least 2 hours. Before serving, decorate the pie with the 2 tablespoons pineapple.

Joan Simon

*Top to bottom: Pineapple Macadamia Cheesepie,
Raspberry Cheesecake Blossoms (page 200)*

Cream cheese is an American original that was developed over a century ago. It was first produced commercially by a farmer in upstate New York and used as a spread on breads, crackers and bagels. Few considered using it in any other way and certainly no one gave a thought to cooking with it. Fortunately, this is no longer true. In fact, cheesecake is now America's third favorite dessert—after apple pie and ice cream.

RASPBERRY CHEESECAKE BLOSSOMS

♦ Finalist in the Dairy Dessert Recipe Contest, sponsored by the Southeast United Dairy Industry Association, Atlanta, Georgia

Makes 12 servings

8 sheets filo dough
4 tablespoons (1/2 stick) butter, melted
1/2 cup cottage cheese
1 (8-ounce) package cream cheese, softened
1 egg
1/2 cup plus 3 tablespoons sugar, divided
4 teaspoons lemon juice, divided
1/2 teaspoon vanilla extract
3 (10-ounce) packages frozen raspberries, thawed and drained with syrup reserved
1 pint fresh raspberries, for decoration
2 kiwifruit, pared and thinly sliced, for decoration

Preheat the oven to 350°F. Grease 12 (2¹/₂-inch) muffin cups. Layer 4 sheets of filo dough, brushing each sheet with melted butter. Repeat with the remaining 4 sheets, forming a separate stack. Cut each stack in half lengthwise and then into thirds crosswise, making 12 squares total. Gently fit each stacked square into a muffin cup, forming a 4-petaled blossom.

Place the cheeses, egg, 3 tablespoons sugar, 1 teaspoon of the lemon juice and the vanilla in a food processor or blender; process until smooth. Divide the filling evenly among the blossom cups. Bake for 10 to 15 minutes or until lightly browned. Carefully remove the blossoms from the muffin cups to a wire rack to cool.

Pour the reserved raspberry syrup into a small saucepan; bring to a boil and cook until reduced to ³/₄ cup. Puree the thawed raspberries in a food processor or blender; press through a sieve into a bowl to remove the seeds. Stir in the raspberry syrup, ¹/₂ cup sugar and remaining 3 teaspoons lemon juice. Refrigerate until needed.

To serve, spoon equal amounts of the raspberry sauce onto 12 dessert plates. Place a cheesecake blossom on each plate. Top the blossoms with equal portions of fresh raspberries and arrange the kiwifruit in the sauce to resemble leaves.

Vienna Taylor
Richmond, Virginia

SUPREME CHOCOLATE CHEESECAKE

♦ Winner in the Philly "Hall of Fame" Recipe Contest, sponsored by Philadelphia Brand® Cream Cheese

Makes 10 to 12 servings

CRUST
16 creme-filled chocolate cookies, crushed (about 1½ cups)
4 tablespoons (½ stick) margarine, melted

FILLING
3 (8-ounce) packages cream cheese, softened
1 (14-ounce) can sweetened condensed milk
3 eggs
1 (12-ounce) package semisweet chocolate chips, melted
2 teaspoons vanilla extract

TOPPING
⅓ cup (⅔ stick) margarine, softened
½ cup powdered sugar
1 cup (6 ounces) semisweet chocolate chips, melted and cooled
2 tablespoons orange-flavored liqueur

A picture-perfect cheesecake has a smooth top. Some cheesecakes will have small cracks around the rim, however, there should never be center cracks. Following are common causes of cracks in cheesecakes:

1. *Overbaking or baking in a too-hot oven*
2. *Overbeating the batter*
3. *Jarring the cake during baking or cooling*
4. *Refrigerating the cake before it's completely cooled*
5. *Wrong pan size*

Preheat the oven to 300°F. Combine the crust ingredients in a small bowl. Press onto the bottom of a 9-inch springform pan; set aside.

To make the filling, beat the cream cheese and milk in a large bowl at medium speed until well blended. Add the eggs, one at a time, mixing well after each addition. Blend in the 12 ounces melted chocolate and the vanilla. Pour the mixture evenly over the prepared crust. Bake for 1 hour and 10 minutes. Loosen the cake from the edge of the pan; cool completely in the pan on a wire rack.

To make the topping, beat the ⅓ cup margarine and the sugar in a small bowl until light and fluffy. Add the 6 ounces melted chocolate and the liqueur, mixing until thoroughly blended. Carefully remove the side of the springform pan. Spread the topping over the top and side of the cheesecake. Refrigerate. Remove from the refrigerator 30 minutes before serving.

Kim Marsden
Renton, Washington

DESSERTS

(continued)

Hazelnuts or filberts have thin brown skins that are often removed before eating. One way to remove the skins is to place the nuts on a baking sheet and bake them in a preheated 350°F oven for 7 to 10 minutes or until the skins begin to flake off. Remove them from the oven, wrap them in a heavy towel and rub them against the towel to remove as much of the skins as possible.

CHOCOLATE MOUSSE ESPRESSO WITH HAZELNUT BRITTLE

♦ Prize-winning recipe in the Knox® Unflavored Gelatine Recipe Contest, sponsored by Thomas J. Lipton, Inc., at The Culinary Institute of America, Hyde Park, New York

Makes about 10 servings

Hazelnut Brittle (recipe follows)
2 envelopes Knox® Unflavored Gelatine
3/4 cup sugar, divided
4 teaspoons instant espresso coffee
2 3/4 cups milk
12 (1-ounce) squares semisweet chocolate
1 1/2 cups heavy cream
2 1/2 cups chocolate cookie wafer crumbs
2/3 cup hazelnuts, toasted, skinned and chopped

Prepare the Hazelnut Brittle; set aside. Mix the gelatine with 1/2 cup of the sugar and the coffee in a medium-sized saucepan; blend in the milk and let stand for 1 minute. Stir over low heat for about 5 minutes or until the gelatine is completely dissolved. Add the chocolate and continue heating, stirring constantly, until the chocolate is melted. Using a wire whisk, beat the mixture until the chocolate is thoroughly blended. Pour the mixture into a large bowl and refrigerate, stirring occasionally, until it mounds slightly when dropped from a spoon.

(continued)

Whip the cream with the remaining ¼ cup sugar in a medium-sized bowl. Reserve ½ cup of the cream for decoration; fold the remainder into the gelatine mixture. Combine the cookie crumbs and the hazelnuts. Alternately layer the gelatine mixture with the hazelnut mixture in parfait glasses or dessert dishes. Refrigerate for at least 30 minutes. Decorate the dishes with the reserved whipped cream and pieces of hazelnut brittle.

HAZELNUT BRITTLE: Toast, skin and chop 1 cup hazelnuts. Place 1 cup sugar in a large skillet over medium heat. As it begins to melt, gently tilt the skillet until the sugar is completely melted and golden brown. Stir in the hazelnuts. Quickly pour the mixture onto a greased baking sheet; let stand until cooled and hardened. Break the brittle into pieces.

Jonathan A. Fox
Wheeling, Illinois

At one time, ripe strawberries were sold at the market threaded through a piece of long straw—maybe this is how they got their name.

THE GOLDEN STRAWBERRY

♦ Prize-winning recipe in the Knox® Unflavored Gelatine Recipe Contest, sponsored by Thomas J. Lipton, Inc., at The Culinary Institute of America, Hyde Park, New York

Makes about 8 servings

   1 envelope Knox® Unflavored Gelatine
   ⅓ cup strawberry-flavored liqueur
   6 ounces Montrachet goat cheese
   4 tablespoons sugar, divided
   ¼ cup sour cream
   2 tablespoons honey
   ½ teaspoon ground cinnamon
   ¼ teaspoon ground nutmeg
   3 egg whites*
   ½ cup heavy cream, whipped
   1 pint strawberries, quartered
   6 ounces amaretti cookies, coarsely crushed (about
       1 cup)
   Whipped cream, for decorating
   Whole strawberries, for decorating
   Whole amaretti cookies, for decorating

Use clean, uncracked eggs.

Sprinkle the gelatine over the liqueur in a small saucepan and let stand for 1 minute. Stir over low heat for about 5 minutes or until the gelatine is completely dissolved. Using a wire whisk, blend in the cheese and 2 tablespoons of the sugar. Pour the mixture into a large bowl and blend in the sour cream, honey, cinnamon and nutmeg; set aside.

Beat the egg whites in a medium-sized bowl until soft peaks form. Gradually add the remaining 2 tablespoons sugar and beat until stiff. Fold the egg whites into the gelatine mixture, then fold in the whipped cream and quartered strawberries. Alternately layer the strawberry mixture with the crushed cookies in parfait glasses or dessert dishes; refrigerate until completely set. Decorate the dishes with additional whipped cream, whole strawberries and cookies.

Kevin P. Dunn
Allegan, Michigan

SIMPLE SPUMONI

♦ Prize winner in a contest run by home economics teachers across the United States, sponsored by the Cherry Marketing Institute, Inc., Okemos, Michigan

Makes about 1 quart

   2 cups whipping cream
²/₃ cup (7 ounces) sweetened condensed milk
¹/₂ teaspoon rum extract
   1 (21-ounce) can cherry pie filling
¹/₂ cup chopped almonds
¹/₂ cup miniature chocolate chips

Combine the whipping cream, milk and rum extract in a large bowl; cover and refrigerate for 30 minutes. Remove from the refrigerator and beat just until soft peaks form. Do not overbeat. Fold in the cherry pie filling, almonds and chocolate chips. Transfer to an 8-inch square pan. Cover and freeze for about 4 hours or until firm. Scoop into dessert dishes and serve.

Jane Saribay
Pahala Elementary School
Pahala, Hawaii

Spumoni is a Sicilian ice cream that is usually flavored with ground almonds and some kind of fruit, such as cherries or lemon. It is lightened with whipped cream or egg whites and is usually served in small portions due to its richness.

Beating Heavy Cream

To obtain the best results when beating heavy or whipping cream, be sure to chill the bowl and beaters first—the coldness keeps the fat in the cream solid, thus increasing the volume. Beating the cream in a deep, narrow bowl also increases the volume. Add flavorings to the cream, such as powdered sugar and vanilla extract, after it has begun to thicken; sweetened whipped cream will have a softer texture than unsweetened.

MAPLE DREAM BARS

♦ Winner of the Mrs. Maple award at the Vermont Maple Festival, St. Albans, Vermont

Makes about 3 dozen bars

2 cups all-purpose flour
1 cup chopped nuts
1 cup (2 sticks) butter, melted
1 cup powdered sugar
1 (8-ounce) package cream cheese, softened
1 cup non-dairy whipped topping
3 cups maple syrup
3 eggs,* lightly beaten
2/3 cup all-purpose flour
1/2 cup water
1/2 teaspoon salt
2 tablespoons butter, chilled, cut into small pieces
1 cup heavy cream, whipped
Pecan halves, for decoration

Preheat the oven to 350°F. Combine the 2 cups flour, the nuts and melted butter in a small bowl; pat onto the bottom of a 13 × 9 × 2-inch pan. Bake for 20 minutes. Set aside to cool slightly. Combine the sugar, cream cheese and non-dairy topping in a medium-sized bowl; blend thoroughly. Spread the mixture on top of the crust.

Pour the maple syrup into the top of a double boiler and warm over hot water. Meanwhile, combine the eggs, the 2/3 cup flour, the water and salt in a small bowl. Beat thoroughly and add to the warm syrup; continue cooking until it boils, beating constantly to prevent sticking. Remove from the heat and add the chilled butter, stirring until it is melted. Let the mixture cool, then spread it over the cheese layer. Spread the whipped cream in a layer over the top and decorate with pecan halves. Cut into 2 × 1 1/2-inch bars.

Use clean, uncracked eggs.

Irene Brousseau

Top to bottom: Simple Spumoni (page 205), Maple Dream Bars

FRUIT SALSA SUNDAES ▶

♦ Grand Prize winner in the "Skinny Dip" Recipe Contest, sponsored by Dreyer's/Edy's Grand Light®

Makes 4 servings

    4 (6-inch) flour tortillas
1¹/₂ cups diced peeled peaches
1¹/₂ cups diced strawberries
    2 tablespoons sugar
    1 tablespoon finely chopped crystallized ginger
¹/₂ teaspoon grated lime rind
    4 (4-ounce) scoops Dreyer's/Edy's Grand Light®
       Vanilla
    Sprigs of fresh mint, for decoration

Preheat the oven to 350°F. Soften the tortillas according to the package directions. Press each one down into an ungreased 10-ounce custard cup. Bake for 10 to 15 minutes or until the tortillas are crisp. Set aside to cool. Combine the peaches, strawberries, sugar, ginger and lime rind in a large bowl; mix gently until well blended. To assemble, remove the tortilla shells from the custard cups; place each on a dessert plate and fill with 1 scoop of Grand Light®. Spoon equal portions of the fruit salsa over the top. Decorate with mint sprigs.

Charlene Margesson

BILOXI BLUEBERRIES SPECIAL

♦ Runner-up in the "Skinny Dip" Recipe Contest, sponsored by Dreyer's/Edy's Grand Light®

Makes 8 servings

    8 (4-ounce) scoops Dreyer's/Edy's Grand Light® New
       York Blueberry Cheesecake
    2 cups fresh or frozen blueberries, thawed if frozen
    1 teaspoon vanilla extract
¹/₂ teaspoon grated lemon rind
1¹/₂ cups plain low-fat yogurt
¹/₂ cup packed brown sugar

Heat the broiler. Place 1 scoop of the Grand Light® in each of 8 individual ovenproof bowls. Spoon ¹/₄ cup blueberries over the top of each. Stir the vanilla and rind into the yogurt; divide evenly over the blueberries. Press the sugar through a sieve over the top. Broil briefly to caramelize the sugar. Serve immediately.

Janet A. Hill

LONE STAR PRALINE ICE CREAM

♦ Food and Wine Award winner at the March of Dimes Gourmet Gala in Dallas, Texas

Makes about 1 gallon

  1 quart milk
  2 vanilla beans, split lengthwise
 12 egg yolks*
  1 cup sugar
  3 cups heavy cream, divided
    Praline Pecans (recipe follows)
  1 teaspoon vanilla extract
  2 teaspoons praline liqueur

Scald the milk in a medium-sized heavy saucepan with the vanilla beans over medium heat. Remove from the heat and set aside. Whisk the egg yolks with the sugar in the top of a double boiler until frothy and lemon colored. Place over simmering water and cook gently, stirring constantly, until the eggs are warmed through. Remove and discard the vanilla beans from the milk. Slowly add the milk and 1 cup of the cream to the egg mixture; cook and stir for about 20 minutes or until the mixture coats the back of a metal spoon. Strain into a clean bowl and set in a larger bowl filled with ice water. Stir until completely cooled.

Prepare the Praline Pecans; set aside. Pour the cooled custard into a chilled ice cream maker. Add the remaining 2 cups cream, the vanilla extract and liqueur. Freeze the mixture according to the manufacturer's directions. When almost frozen, add 1¹/₂ cups of the praline pecans and freeze completely. Serve the ice cream decorated with the remaining pecans.

PRALINE PECANS: Heat ²/₃ cup *each* sugar and praline liqueur in a large heavy skillet over low heat until the sugar dissolves. Stir in 2 cups pecans, broken, and continue to cook until all the liquid has evaporated; cool.

Use clean, uncracked eggs.

Mr. and Mrs. Stephen T. Winn

The flavor of vanilla beans is highly superior to the flavor of vanilla extract. The beans are actually seed pods of a certain variety of orchid and the vanilla essence lies inside the beans in hundreds of tiny black seeds. To infuse a custard sauce or ice cream with the taste of vanilla, split the beans lengthwise with the point of a paring knife. The split beans may be steeped in the sauce and then removed, or the seeds may be scraped out and left in the sauce. You will see small flecks of vanilla seeds in some high-quality vanilla ice creams.

CREAMY ORANGE ICE CREAM

♦ Finalist in the Dairy Dessert Recipe Contest, sponsored by the Southeast United Dairy Industry Association, Atlanta, Georgia

Makes 1¹/2 quarts

  4 egg yolks*
²/3 cup sugar
  1 cup half-and-half
  1 cup freshly squeezed orange juice, strained (3 to
    4 large oranges)
1¹/2 teaspoons grated orange rind
  4 tablespoons (¹/2 stick) butter, cut into 4 pieces
  1 cup heavy cream
¹/2 teaspoon vanilla extract
¹/2 teaspoon orange extract
  Red and yellow food colorings (optional)

*W*ay back in days gone by, there were few things in life as glorious as homemade ice cream. However, trudging out to the kitchen to make the ice cream was decidedly less than glorious. Fortunately, the many new ice cream makers on the market today have made the task of preparing homemade ice cream as easy as pie.

Beat the egg yolks and sugar in a medium-sized bowl until thickened and pale. Heat the half-and-half, orange juice and orange rind in a medium-sized heavy saucepan over medium-low heat until bubbles rise (about 180°F on a candy thermometer). *Do not boil.* Gradually add the warm orange juice mixture to the egg mixture, whisking constantly. Pour the mixture back into the saucepan. Place over medium-low heat and cook, stirring constantly, until the mixture begins to thicken. *Do not boil.* Remove the pan from the heat and add the butter, stirring until all the pieces have melted. Pour the mixture into a bowl and cover. Place inside a larger bowl that contains ice and water. Set in the freezer to cool for about 45 minutes, stirring occasionally.

Combine the heavy cream, vanilla and orange extract in a small bowl; whip until stiff peaks form. Fold into the cooled orange juice mixture and add the food colorings to make an orange color, if desired. Freeze the mixture in an ice cream maker according to the manufacturer's directions. When the ice cream is frozen, transfer it to a bowl. Cover and freeze overnight. Let the ice cream soften in the refrigerator for about 30 minutes before serving.

*Use clean, uncracked eggs.

Bob Borzak
Nashville, Tennessee

APRICOT ROLL-UPS

♦ Winner of the Apricot Sweepstakes at the Patterson Apricot Fiesta, sponsored by the Apricot Advisory Board, Walnut Creek, California

Makes 20 to 26 roll-ups

> 4 cups dried apricots
> 1 (12-ounce) can apricot-pineapple nectar
> 1¹/₂ cups water
> ¹/₂ cup sugar
> 2 tablespoons lemon juice
> 1 tablespoon quick-cooking tapioca
> 2 cups finely chopped walnuts
> 1 (7-ounce) package shredded coconut
> 1 package egg roll wrappers
> Vegetable oil, for frying
> Powdered sugar, for dusting
> Sour cream, for dipping
> Chocolate sauce, for dipping

Combine the apricots, nectar, water, sugar and lemon juice in a large saucepan; bring to a boil. Remove from the heat; cover and let stand for 1 hour. Drain the mixture, reserving the liquid. Chop the apricots finely. Combine the chopped apricots, reserved liquid and tapioca in the same saucepan; bring to a boil, stirring constantly. Remove from the heat and let stand for 20 minutes. Stir in the walnuts and coconut.

For each roll-up, place about 2 heaping tablespoons of the apricot mixture on the lower half of an egg roll wrapper. Moisten the left and right edges with water. Fold the bottom edge up to just cover the filling. Fold the left and right edges ¹/₂ inch over; roll up jelly-roll fashion. Moisten the top edge and seal.

Heat about 2 inches of the oil in a heavy skillet to 370°F. Place a few rolls at a time, seam side down, in the hot oil. Fry until golden brown all over, turning the rolls as necessary; drain on paper towels. Dust with powdered sugar. Serve the roll-ups with bowls of sour cream and chocolate sauce for dipping.

Harriet Kuhn
Patterson, California

Unsweetened cocoa is formed by extracting most of the cocoa butter from pure chocolate and grinding the remaining chocolate solids into a powder. "Dutch process" cocoa is unsweetened cocoa that has been treated with an alkali, giving it a darker appearance and a slightly less bitter flavor. In recipes, do not substitute sweetened cocoa, the type that is used for making hot chocolate, for unsweetened cocoa.

CHOCOLATE ALMOND LADYFINGER CROWN

♦ Second place in the Chocolate Specialties category in the Chocolate Recipe Contest, sponsored by Lexington Market, Inc., Baltimore, Maryland

Makes about 12 servings

> 2 envelopes unflavored gelatine
> 1¼ cups granulated sugar, divided
> ¾ cup unsweetened cocoa
> 4 eggs,* separated
> 2¼ cups milk
> ⅓ cup almond-flavored liqueur
> 2 (3-ounce) packages ladyfingers, split
> 1½ cups heavy cream, whipped
>   Almond Cream (recipe follows)
>   Sliced almonds, for decoration

Mix the gelatine with 1 cup of the granulated sugar and the cocoa in a medium-sized saucepan. Blend in the egg yolks beaten with the milk and let stand for 1 minute. Stir over low heat for about 5 minutes or until the gelatine is completely dissolved. Using a wire whisk, beat the mixture until the cocoa is completely blended, then stir in the liqueur. Pour into a large bowl and refrigerate, stirring occasionally, until the mixture mounds slightly when dropped from a spoon. Meanwhile, line the bottom and side of a 9-inch springform pan with split ladyfingers and refrigerate.

Beat the egg whites in a large bowl until soft peaks form. Gradually add the remaining ¼ cup granulated sugar and beat until stiff. Fold the egg whites into the gelatine mixture, then fold in the whipped cream. Pour the mixture into the prepared pan and refrigerate until firm. To serve, remove the side of the springform pan. Decorate with Almond Cream and sliced almonds.

Use clean, uncracked eggs.

ALMOND CREAM: Beat ½ cup heavy cream with 1 tablespoon powdered sugar in a small bowl until stiff. Fold in 1 tablespoon almond-flavored liqueur.

Jill Earl
Baltimore, Maryland

LEMON SPONGE PUDDING

♦ Prize-winning recipe at the March of Dimes Gourmet Gala in Pittsburgh, Pennsylvania

Serves 6

   4 tablespoons (¹/₂ stick) unsalted butter
  ¹/₄ cup granulated sugar
   3 eggs, separated
  ¹/₃ cup lemon juice
  ¹/₃ cup all-purpose flour
   1 tablespoon grated lemon rind
  ¹/₄ teaspoon salt
  1¹/₂ cups milk
      Pinch of cream of tartar
      Powdered sugar, for decoration
      Lemon rind, for garnish

Preheat the oven to 350°F. Cream the butter and granulated sugar in a large bowl. Add the egg yolks, one at a time, beating well after each addition. Beat in the lemon juice, flour, lemon rind and salt. Add the milk in a steady stream, beating and combining the mixture well.

Beat the egg whites with the cream of tartar in a medium-sized bowl until stiff peaks form. Stir one fourth of the egg whites into the lemon mixture. Gently, but thoroughly, fold in the remaining whites. Pour the mixture into a 1¹/₂-quart soufflé dish. Set the dish in a deep pan and pour boiling water into the pan to come halfway up the sides of the dish. Bake for about 50 minutes or until puffed and golden brown on the top. Sift the powdered sugar over the top. Serve warm or chilled; garnish with lemon rind.

Note: The sponge will separate, forming a custardlike sauce on the bottom of the dish.

Elsie Hillman

Slow-cooking foods, such as custards, pâtés and soufflés, are usually baked in hot water baths. The baking dish is placed in a larger container that is filled halfway with hot, often boiling, water. During baking, the hot water bath provides a constant, steady heat source to the food, ensuring it will cook evenly.